VEGETARIAN
COOKBOOK

VEGETARIAN
COOKBOOK

PAUL GAYLER

Photography by Philip Wilkins

A Dorling Kindersley Book

Dorling **DK** Kindersley

LONDON, NEW YORK, SYDNEY, DELHI, PARIS
MUNICH and JOHANNESBURG

*For the new-age vegetarians who
demand quality, taste, and innovation*

Project Editor Jo Younger

Art Editor Julia Worth

Editor Nicky Vimpany

Designer Laura Jackson

DTP Designer Bridget Roseberry

Senior Managing Editor Krystyna Mayer

Deputy Art Director Carole Ash

Production Manager Maryann Webster

Home Economist Jane Suthering

First published in Great Britain in 1999
by Dorling Kindersley Limited,
9 Henrietta Street, London WC2E 8PS

First published as a Dorling Kindersley paperback 2000
2 4 6 8 10 9 7 5 3 1

Copyright © 1999, 2000 Dorling Kindersley Limited, London
Text copyright © 1999, 2000 Paul Gayler

A CIP catalogue for this book is available from the British Library.

ISBN 0 7513 2918 5

Reproduced by GRB Editrice, Verona
Printed and bound in Singapore by Star Standard Industries (Pte.) Ltd.

—————— POINTS TO REMEMBER ——————

All spoon measurements are level unless otherwise stated. Always
follow either metric or imperial measurements, never mix the
two. Eggs are medium unless otherwise stated. Milk is full-fat
milk unless otherwise stated. The nutritional notes give values per
portion and are an estimate only, based on average values. For
fan ovens, oven temperatures should be adjusted according to
the manufacturer's instructions. Some of the cheeses in this book
may be made with animal rennet. Strict vegetarians may wish to
substitute cheeses made with vegetarian rennet where appropriate.

see our complete
catalogue at
www.dk.com

CONTENTS

INTRODUCTION 6

GALLERY

*A visual preview of versatile vegetarian
cuisine, from sophisticated soups and
stuffed vegetables, through tarts and pies, to
shamelessly indulgent desserts.*

INGREDIENTS

A guide to all the essential basic ingredients for the modern vegetarian cook plus a few exotic extras to spice up your repertoire, with information on choosing, storing, and cooking.

EQUIPMENT & TECHNIQUES

How to choose and use equipment for vegetarian cookery, plus a step-by-step guide to all the essential basic techniques.

RECIPES

Over 140 creative and delicious recipes to suit every occasion, with influences from every corner of the globe, which will inspire everyone who loves good food.

INTRODUCTION

IT IS NEARLY 15 YEARS since I devised my first vegetarian menu and offered it alongside the conventional one at Inigo Jones, the London restaurant where I worked as chef director. At that time, vegetarianism and *haute cuisine* were considered two culinary extremes, never destined to meet on the same plate. Today the tables have turned, and it is rare to find a restaurant that does not include a vegetarian option on its menu. Over the last decade there has been a quiet revolution in the way we eat: traditional meal structures have broken down; ingredients that were once considered exotic are now commonplace; and vegetarian food has been accepted as part of the mainstream.

THE MODERN VEGETARIAN

Leaf through the vegetarian cook books of 20 years ago and you will find a depressing list of worthy, but dull culinary staples: wholemeal flour, brown rice, lentils, root vegetables, and lots of nuts. These were served up in relentlessly heavy and unpalatable combinations with nothing to relieve them. Nowadays, many vegetarian staples have been taken up by chefs and cookery writers, with spectacular results. Lentils, for example, are wildly fashionable, particularly the tiny, slate-blue Puy lentils from France. These are combined with sophisticated flavourings such as balsamic vinegar, herbs, and truffles. Root vegetables are roasted to bring out their natural sweetness, or mixed to a rich, unctuous purée with cream or olive oil. Substitute ingredients such as margarine and carob are being dropped and replaced by the real thing. After all, why shouldn't vegetarians enjoy good butter and quality chocolate? I'm more interested in creating sophisticated vegetarian food that has depth of flavour. This isn't difficult to achieve. Dried mushrooms and tomato concentrates, Oriental seasonings such as soy sauce, high-quality olive oils, and various cooking pastes such as tapenade and harissa, are staples in the modern kitchen, and all of these are appropriate ingredients for vegetarian recipes.

THE GLOBAL KITCHEN

The dazzling array of ingredients now available from all over the world has led to an explosion of interest in cooking. The fact that we can go into supermarkets now and pick up Oriental herbs alongside French dairy products and Mexican salsas has made us all into culinary magpies, mixing and matching cooking styles and ingredients. Done with restraint and a respect for flavours, this innovative way of eating can be incredibly exciting. It has opened up a whole new world of vegetarian cuisine in which a Spanish gazpacho can be flavoured with mild spices, pesto can be made with goat's cheese, and a risotto can be flavoured with Thai ingredients such as lemongrass, coconut, and coriander.

COOKING FOR THE FUTURE

I find that vegetarian food works best if you concentrate on providing a harmonious balance of flavours, textures, and colours. Although you can still cook a central dish if that is how you like to eat, it is often easier and more appropriate to prepare a selection of lighter dishes. This way of eating is nothing new in the Middle East, India, and the Far East, and I find these cuisines a continual source of inspiration. My cooking has not been immune to the Mediterranean fever that has swept the United Kingdom and North America either. Mediterranean influences are here to stay and the food of Italy, in particular, has had a lasting impact on the way we eat. This is great news for vegetarians, for surely no other nation has created so many imaginative vegetable dishes as the Italians, not to mention all the meatless pasta sauces and risottos. Unlike Italian cooking, French cuisine is not rich in vegetarian dishes. However, I believe that classic French cooking techniques can be applied to an exciting range of global ingredients, giving a new refinement to vegetarian cooking. In devising recipes for this book I have been able to experiment with the pick of the best produce from all over the world. Whether you are a committed vegetarian or a confirmed carnivore I think you will be as gratified as I was to discover how diverse and exciting modern vegetarian cooking can be. From Mardi Gras Jambalaya to Parsnip and Wild Rice Mulligatawny, Asian Noodle Salad to Tuscan Roll, I hope this book has something to delight anyone who loves good food.

Paul Gayler

GALLERY

THIS INSPIRATIONAL GALLERY OF VEGETARIAN DISHES
IS DESIGNED TO TANTALIZE EVERY SENSE:
STUFFED VEGETABLES, OOZING WITH FLAVOUR, ALFRESCO
FOOD SIZZLING OVER HOT COALS, LUSCIOUS DESSERTS
DRIPPING WITH FRUIT, AND SO MUCH MORE. USE THESE PAGES
TO GET A TASTE OF THE TREATS THAT LIE IN STORE IN
THE RECIPE SECTION, OR TO PLAN A MENU TO TEMPT YOUR
FRIENDS OR INDULGE YOURSELF.

SOUPS

Above and opposite
CHILLED CUCUMBER & BULGAR WHEAT SOUP *(see page 65)*

BECAUSE SOUPS CAN BE PREPARED well in advance, they are ideal for serving at dinner parties, for special occasions, or for quick lunches. Presentation is all important. With a few garnishes you can transform a soup into something special. Whether it is a light, cold consommé or a more warming brew, soup can make an impressive starter, or be a complete meal in itself.

"It's good soup and not fine words that keeps me alive."

Molière, playwright, 1672

PARSNIP & WILD RICE MULLIGATAWNY *(see page 61)*

EARLY SUMMER BASIL SOUP *(see page 60)*

CHICKPEA & CHARD MINESTRONE WITH PESTO *(see page 60)*

– here are soups for all seasons – satisfying winter warmers to Refreshing, cool, smooth summer revivers

STUFFED VEGETABLES

Above and opposite
STUFFED GOLDEN & RED
PEPPERS *(see page 113)*

THERE IS SOMETHING very satisfying about preparing vegetables to be stuffed and the process is relatively simple, too. Stuffings can consist of just a few carefully chosen ingredients simply thrown together, or they can be more elaborate and prepared with greater care for more sumptuous effects. Whatever the aim – a quick and simple light lunch or a dinner party show-stopper – I hope these recipes will provide the inspiration.

"... Taste the fruit and resign yourself to the influences of each."

Henry David Thoreau, essayist, naturalist, and poet, 1817–1862

ORIENTAL
STUFFED
AUBERGINES
(see page 110)

Dramatic centrepieces, these vegetables are bursting with flavour

GEM SQUASH
WITH TOFU
(see page 108)

STUFFED
ROAST ONIONS
(see page 111)

ALFRESCO FOOD

COOKING IN THE FRESH AIR over hot coals imparts a delicious smoky taste to food. With a little imagination you can produce an impressive vegetarian barbecue spread. Here, succulent vegetables and spicy marinades, and juicy chunks of fruit infused with the subtle flavour of lemongrass are combined with the chargrill flavours of spiced corn and aromatic herby tomatoes.

"A man hath no better thing under the sun, than to eat, and to drink, and to be merry."

Ecclesiastes,
Old Testament, 977 BC

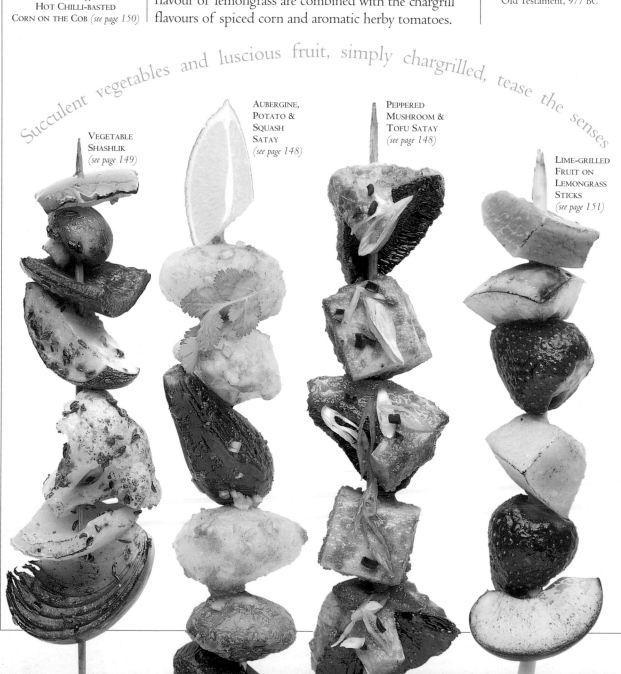

Above and opposite
HOT CHILLI-BASTED
CORN ON THE COB *(see page 150)*

Succulent vegetables and luscious fruit, simply chargrilled, tease the senses

VEGETABLE
SHASHLIK
(see page 149)

AUBERGINE,
POTATO &
SQUASH
SATAY
(see page 148)

PEPPERED
MUSHROOM &
TOFU SATAY
(see page 148)

LIME-GRILLED
FRUIT ON
LEMONGRASS
STICKS
(see page 151)

TARTS & PIES

CRISP, DELICATE PASTRY makes a perfect wrapping for an infinite variety of fillings. Here, I have built up high-rise pies that slice open to reveal colourful layers of ingredients, and created delicious fillings for delicate filo pastry and intriguing pastry parcels that are impressive enough for a celebratory meal. There are pastries for family picnics through to sophisticated suppers.

"What is a roofless cathedral compared to a well-built pie?"

William Maginn, poet, 1794–1842

Above and opposite
CEP, WALNUT & JERUSALEM
ARTICHOKE PARCELS *(see page 73)*

SPINACH, BASIL & PUMPKIN
RICE TORTE *(see page 68)*

HIGH-RISE PASTA PIE
(see page 71)

CARROT & BEAN PIE WITH
THYME CREAM *(see page 152)*

Light and crisp pastry, filled with colourful layers of exciting flavours

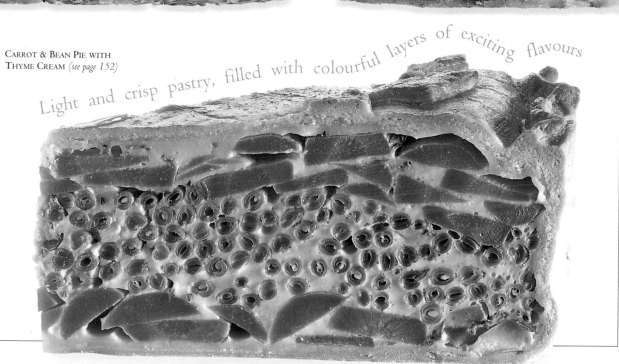

STACKS

THESE STACKS ARE PILED HIGH with flavour. Here, two starters, a salad, and a main course have all been built up using ingredients with contrasting colours and textures, and with the flavours of the Orient, Mediterranean, and Middle East. The recipes are simple to follow and, with a little patience, these gastronomic sculptures are easy to achieve. Flourishes of leaves add the finishing touches.

"If one has the art, then a piece of celery or salted cabbage can be made into a marvellous delicacy."

Yuan Mei, Chinese poet, 18th century

Above and opposite
CAPONATA ON ROASTED GARLIC BRUSCHETTA *(see page 50)*

STACKED VEGETABLE CEVICHE *(see page 54)*

TOASTED MILLET & CUMIN VEGETABLES *(see page 103)*

The art of presentation reaches new heights: these culinary creations are truly gastronomic treats

SINGAPORE NOODLE SALAD *(see page 120)*

DESERTS

EVERYONE LOVES DESSERTS. I have included recipes for unusual, sweet, vegetable desserts, more conventional crème caramels, and crisp, refreshing ices. Some recipes are simple to prepare, and others need a little more time and attention to achieve the end result. I have tried to incorporate a selection of desserts to suit every taste, making full use of the diversity of ingredients available.

"I like to shock people — especially with dessert... If you really know the classics, then you can vary as you like."

Charles Palmer, chef, 20th century

Above and opposite
HAZELNUT TORTE WITH KIRSCH & BLUEBERRIES
(see page 126)

FROZEN LEMON YOGURT & PEPPER CHERRIES
(see page 133)

ITALIAN CREME CARAMEL
(see page 135)

Mouthwatering desserts with cascades of fruit and pools of sauce dazzle the eye

BUTTERNUT SOUFFLE WITH BLACKBERRIES *(see page 131)*

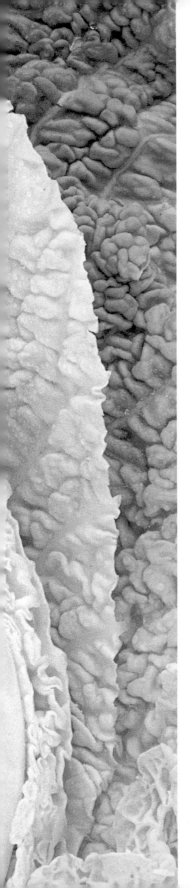

INGREDIENTS

HERE IS AN ILLUSTRATED GUIDE TO THE CORNUCOPIA
OF FRESH INGREDIENTS AVAILABLE TO VEGETARIANS TODAY,
WITH ADVICE ON SELECTION, STORAGE, AND
PREPARATION. ALL FRESH PRODUCE IS AT ITS BEST EATEN AS
SOON AS POSSIBLE AFTER PURCHASE, SO MAKE THE
MOST OF LOCAL SHOPS, MARKETS, AND DELICATESSENS
TO BUY LITTLE AND OFTEN, RATHER THAN STORING
INGREDIENTS FOR A LONG TIME.

SHOOTS, PODS & SEEDS

PODS AND SEEDS are packed with nutrients, and provide protein and fibre. Shoots contain small amounts of vitamins, and add wonderful flavours and textures to dishes.

FENNEL has a lovely, sweet, aniseed flavour. Buy plump bulbs. After cutting, drop them into water with a little lemon juice to prevent them from discolouring.

ARTICHOKES are a real treat, well worth the trouble they take to prepare. They have a subtle, earthy flavour and can be boiled or baked. Serve them hot or cold.

ASPARAGUS should have tight buds and tender stems. Cook them in a bundle, standing in 2.5cm (1 inch) water. Cover with foil to keep the steam in.

CELERY stalks should snap easily; soft stalks indicate that the celery is past its best. It is excellent raw in salads, and with dips or cheese, and can be braised or used in soups and stocks.

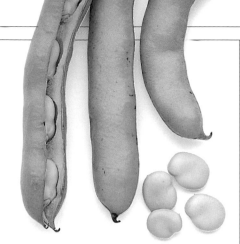

BROAD BEANS can be topped and tailed and eaten in the pod when young and tender. If they are tougher, remove from the pods, cook in boiling water, and rub off the skins.

OKRA is pungent and slightly glutinous. Buy pods that will snap, not bend, and trim the stalks before cooking. Okra is good in most stews, curries, and rice dishes.

BABY CORN comes from the same plant as sweetcorn, but is picked young. It is excellent in stir-fries; add it whole or cut in half lengthways and cook for just a few minutes.

SWEETCORN is best soon after picking. Look for creamy, tightly packed kernels. Strip off the husks and boil or barbecue; do not add salt since it will toughen the kernels.

MANGETOUTS are immature peas that are eaten complete with the pod. Bright, flat, fresh-looking pods with slight swellings are best. Cook briefly in boiling water or stir-fry.

FRESH PEAS are more widely available than they used to be; the pods should be bright and full, but not hard. Pop peas out of the pods and cook briefly in boiling water.

BRASSICAS & LEAVES

GREEN LEAFY VEGETABLES contain valuable amounts of vitamins A, B, and C, as well as fibre, iron, and calcium. They keep well for about three days in the salad drawer of the refrigerator. Serve salad leaves and brassicas raw or lightly cooked to preserve their nutrients.

PAK CHOI has a delicate, mild flavour and is used in many Asian dishes. For the best results, stir-fry or steam pak choi for the shortest possible time.

KOHLRABI is crisp with a nutty flavour. Buy the smallest you can find; the youngest can be sliced and stir-fried, otherwise steam for 15–20 minutes, then peel.

CHINESE LEAF is a succulent cabbage with a delicate flavour. It is excellent in stir-fries and soups, as well as raw. It keeps for about a week in the refrigerator.

SAVOY CABBAGE is packed with flavour. Look for a firm cabbage with crisp leaves that are dark outside and paler inside. It is delicious cooked slowly with a little butter.

RED CHARD *is delicate and distinctive enough to serve on its own like asparagus. Choose young, tender leaves and steam them lightly to retain their flavour.*

RADICCHIO *is popular for adding colour and texture to salads, although it can also be cooked. It has a slightly bitter flavour. Buy bright, crisp, unblemished leaves.*

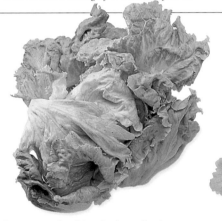

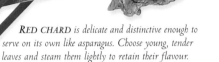

BATAVIA *is a broad-leaved endive with a characteristic, slightly bitter flavour. The leaves are either pale green or red-tinged and make an interesting addition to salads.*

ROCKET *has a distinctive, peppery taste and can be added to salads or stirred into pasta sauces. Select bright leaves with no yellowing.*

CHICORY *is sometimes called by its French name, endive. Look for tightly packed leaves and break them apart to use in salads, braise whole, or serve hot with a cheese sauce.*

FRISEE *is a slightly bitter salad leaf that is both decorative and tasty. Buy frisée with a crisp, light green central core of leaves and use as fresh as possible.*

FRUIT VEGETABLES & SQUASHES

PEPPERS AND TOMATOES contain more vitamin C than many fruits, and squashes contain useful amounts of vitamin A. Fruit vegetables should be stored in the refrigerator, while squashes will keep well in a cool place.

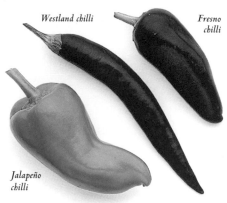

Westland chilli

Fresno chilli

Jalapeño chilli

CHILLIES *are available in different colours, shapes, and sizes. As a rule, the smaller the chilli, the hotter it is. Protect your hands when handling chillies to avoid irritation.*

Plum tomato

Vine tomatoes

Yellow cherry tomatoes

Red tomato

TOMATOES, *whether red or yellow, should be firm, bright, and plump. Plum tomatoes have the sweetest, most intense flavour and are particularly good for sauces.*

AUBERGINES *should have a green stalk and be shiny and plump, with no wrinkles or bruises. They can be stuffed, cooked in casseroles, stews, and bakes, or puréed for using in dips.*

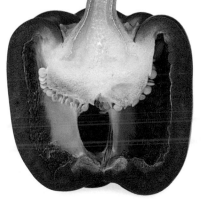

PEPPERS *are available in many colours. Red, yellow, and orange varieties are sweeter than green ones. Use peppers in stir-fries and salads, or try stuffing or roasting them.*

CHRISTOPHENES (CHO-CHO) *have a bland taste that complements stronger flavours. Choose the smallest ones you can find. They can be boiled, baked, fried, or stuffed.*

GEM SQUASH *are excellent for individual servings and can be stuffed and roasted. Alternatively, dice the flesh and use it in the same way as that of any other squash.*

BUTTERNUT SQUASH *have a rich, buttery flavour that gives them their name. Choose firm, unblemished specimens, and use them in casseroles, soups, stews, and purées.*

PUMPKIN *is the most familiar of the squash family. Buy small whole ones in preference to slices.*

ONIONS & MUSHROOMS

ONIONS are familiar ingredients that can help protect against heart disease by lowering cholesterol. Wild mushrooms are less familiar, but are now becoming more readily available. They have a delicious flavour and are an important source of B vitamins for vegetarians.

GARLIC *is an indispensable flavouring that can be added to many dishes, and is also delicious roasted and served whole. Choose firm, fat bulbs with no sign of shooting.*

RED ONIONS *are milder and sweeter than most brown varieties, and are delicious served raw in salads. They retain their colour well, even when cooked.*

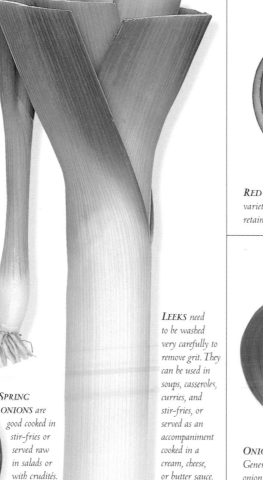

SPRING ONIONS *are good cooked in stir-fries or served raw in salads or with crudités.*

LEEKS *need to be washed very carefully to remove grit. They can be used in soups, casseroles, curries, and stir-fries, or served as an accompaniment cooked in a cream, cheese, or butter sauce.*

ONIONS *vary in strength. Generally, the larger the onion, the milder the taste.*

SHALLOTS *are small, sweet onions, with a more delicate flavour than large onions.*

OPEN-CUP MUSHROOMS *are cultivated mushrooms at a fairly late stage of development, when they are fully open. They are the ideal size for stuffing and baking.*

CHANTERELLES *are one of the most attractive mushrooms. Brush and rinse them, then cook gently in butter and cream to prevent toughening, or add to casseroles.*

SHIITAKE MUSHROOMS *should simply be wiped with kitchen paper before slicing, frying, and adding to rice dishes or stews. They are available fresh and dried.*

OYSTER MUSHROOMS *should be torn into long strips, or used whole if small. They have a strong flavour and a firm texture, and are good in casseroles and Oriental dishes.*

CEPS *are one of the tastiest mushrooms available, with a deep, rich flavour. Add a few to cultivated mushroom dishes to intensify the flavour. Porcini are dried ceps.*

MORELS *have a distinctive look and a strong, meaty taste and smell. Wash them well in salty water to remove dirt from the caps. They are available fresh and dried.*

HERBS & SPICES

FRESH HERBS really bring an extra dimension to many dishes. They should be used as soon as possible after buying or picking since they deteriorate quickly. Buy spices in small quantities and where possible buy them whole, then grind them yourself for the best flavour.

PARSLEY is available in two varieties, flatleaf and curly. Flatleaf parsley has a finer, more robust flavour than curly parsley. Both are used widely to add flavour to many dishes.

BASIL blends well with tomatoes and garlic. Its delicate leaves should be treated with care to prevent bruising, and are usually added to dishes at the end of the cooking time.

THYME is particularly pungent when fresh, and aids the digestion of fatty foods. It is a popular addition to bouquet garni, and is robust enough to withstand long, slow cooking.

CORIANDER has a fresh, citrus-like aroma and taste, and is very popular in Asian and Mexican cookery. It can be used with chillies or yogurt in chutneys, relishes, and salsas.

MINT has a distinctive, refreshing flavour and can aid digestion. This versatile herb can be combined with sweet or savoury ingredients and is delicious with chocolate.

CAYENNE *is made from one of the hottest varieties of chilli. It is used to give heat to sauces, curries, and stews.*

CHILLI FLAKES *are crushed, dried chillies and include lots of seeds. They are very hot, so should be used with caution.*

PAPRIKA *is sweet and mild, with a subtle, peppery taste. It gives warmth and colour to stews and sauces.*

CINNAMON *is a warm, fragrant spice used in sweet and savoury dishes.*

LEMONGRASS *has a fresh citrus scent and is popular in Thai dishes.*

FRESH ROOT GINGER *has a spicy, lemony taste, which is far superior to that of dried ginger. It is most often used in Asian and Indian curries and in sweet dishes.*

CLOVES *are sweet and highly aromatic. They go very well with fruit.*

NUTMEG *has a warm, pungent flavour, and is best used freshly grated.*

STAR ANISE *imparts a sweet, aniseed aroma and looks attractive.*

SAFFRON *is aromatic and tastes slightly bitter. It is often used in rice dishes.*

EQUIPMENT
&
TECHNIQUES

ANY ARTIST NEEDS GOOD TOOLS AND SOUND WORKING
PRACTICES, AND A COOK IS NO EXCEPTION. CHOOSING
EQUIPMENT CAREFULLY AND FOLLOWING A FEW BASIC RULES
FOR PREPARING AND COOKING INGREDIENTS CAN REALLY
MAKE A DIFFERENCE TO A RECIPE. THE FOLLOWING PAGES
PROVIDE A VISUAL CATALOGUE OF THE MOST USEFUL
EQUIPMENT AND TECHNIQUES FOR A VEGETARIAN COOK.

EQUIPMENT

THERE IS AN ENORMOUS RANGE of kitchen equipment available and it can be difficult to know what you really need. Here are some of the things that a vegetarian cook will find most useful. You do not need a lot of equipment, just buy the best quality you can – your cooking will benefit, and you will find that preparation will be much quicker and easier. If you keep your equipment scrupulously clean and dry and your knives sharp, and store everything carefully, these tools should last you a lifetime.

SLOTTED SPOON *This holed spoon is indispensable for skimming stocks and sauces, and for lifting solid food from boiling liquid.*

LADLE *A ladle is useful for serving soups and stews, and for measuring out batter for making pancakes.*

VEGETABLE PEELER *A good peeler will shave a thinner layer of skin than a knife and so preserve more nutrients.*

GARLIC CRUSHER *Easier to use than a knife for crushing garlic, a garlic crusher should ideally have a detachable grille for easy cleaning.*

DARIOLE MOULD *These small, deep-sided moulds are used for shaping pastries, desserts, rice, and noodles.*

TARTLET TIN *These tins are ideal for making individual tarts or quiches. The best are non-stick ones.*

RAMEKIN *Individual servings can be brought straight from the oven to the table in these small ceramic dishes.*

SKEWERS *Metal or bamboo skewers can be used to skewer vegetables for barbecuing, and to prick cakes and pies to test them for doneness.*

BAKING SHEET *A baking sheet should be sturdy and should not bend in your hand. A non-stick surface is useful, but not essential.*

ROASTING TIN *A good-quality, non-stick roasting tin has many uses, from roasting vegetables to setting polenta.*

SPRINGFORM CAKE TIN *This loose-bottomed tin is useful for delicate cakes and can also be used for raised pies.*

CHOPPING BOARD *A wooden board is kinder to knives than other surfaces. It should never be soaked or submerged in water.*

CHEF'S KNIFE *A chef's knife is indispensable for chopping. It should be well balanced with a deep, curved blade.*

PARING KNIFE *Used for paring, peeling, and scraping, a paring knife should be light, with a handle that is comfortable to hold.*

SAUCEPAN *It is well worth investing in good pans. A stainless steel pan is durable and easy to clean, but look for one that has copper or aluminium sandwiched into the base to help conduct heat evenly.*

SIEVE *A sieve has a multitude of uses, from sifting flour to straining stocks and soups and puréeing fruit. The best sieves are made from stainless steel, which does not corrode.*

FRYING PAN
A large, non-stick, heavy-bottomed pan with sloping sides is the best all-round choice. Use it for sautéeing vegetables and cooking omelettes and pancakes.

KITCHEN GADGETS

BLENDER
Ingredients for soups, dips, sauces, and drinks can be puréed in a blender.

FOOD PROCESSOR
This does the job of a blender plus much more. Different blades can chop, mix, grate, and shred.

HAND-HELD BLENDER
This hand-held blender is useful for puréeing food in a pan. It is compact and saves on storage space and washing up — always a bonus.

PASTA MACHINE *These useful machines roll pasta dough out thinly, kneading it as they do so. The best ones are made from chrome-plated steel.*

TECHNIQUES

PREPARING INGREDIENTS in the correct way ensures the best results and helps to cut down on preparation time. These simple techniques show how to get the best from ingredients with the minimum of fuss and waste. Always keep your utensils clean and use a sharp knife for cutting. The method for roasting peppers shown opposite is the easiest and quickest; if you prefer, you can roast peppers in a moderately hot oven for about 40 minutes until blackened, then prepare as shown.

CUTTING VEGETABLES

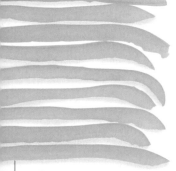

Julienne of pepper

Chopped red onion

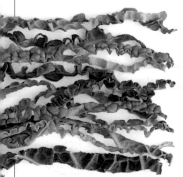

Shredded savoy cabbage

MAKING JULIENNE STRIPS

1 Cut each pepper into quarters, then cut out the stalk, core, and seeds.

2 Slice along the insides of the pepper pieces to remove the white membrane.

3 Hold the pepper pieces skin-side down and slice in long, narrow strips.

CHOPPING AN ONION

1 Peel the onion and trim the top. Cut in half, then slice horizontally, leaving the root intact to hold the slices together.

2 Keep the onion cut-side down on a board, and slice through it, this time vertically, up to, but not through the root.

3 Slice the onion vertically again, making the cuts at right angles to the first set, so that the onion falls away in dice.

SHREDDING CABBAGE

1 Remove the outer leaves and, starting at the narrowest point, roll up each one tightly into a cigar shape.

2 Lay each rolled-up leaf on a work surface and cut across the roll to produce fine shreds of leaf.

3 Cut the remaining cabbage into quarters, cut the core out of each quarter, and slice across the leaves in fine shreds.

CUTTING HERBS

CHOPPING HERBS
Place the herbs on a chopping board. Rock a chef's knife up and down a few times across the leaves to chop them. Delicate herbs, such as basil, should be rolled and shredded in the same way as cabbage leaves (see left).

SNIPPING HERBS & PREPARING FRESH THYME
Hold a bunch of herbs over a bowl and snip into pieces with kitchen scissors, or place the herbs in a bowl and snip with the scissors. Strip the thyme leaves from the stalk before use.

MAKING A BOUQUET GARNI
A bouquet garni can be made with any herbs, and vegetables can also be added. This one was made by tying together thyme sprigs, a bay leaf, and celery stalks with a piece of plain string.

PREPARING & CHOPPING VEGETABLES

ROASTING PEPPERS

1 Cook the peppers whole under a preheated grill for 10–12 minutes until blackened.

2 Transfer to a plastic bag, seal, and cool. Remove the peppers and peel off the skins.

3 Pull out the cores of the peppers, cut each one in half, and scrape out the seeds.

Roasted red pepper strips

CHOPPING GINGER

CHOPPING GARLIC

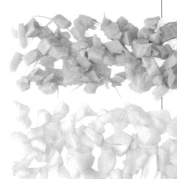

1 Carefully peel the ginger with a paring knife, then cut it into very thin slices, cutting across the grain.

2 Crush the ginger under the flat side of a chef's knife. Place in a pile and cut across the ginger to chop it finely.

Crush the garlic clove under the flat side of a chef's knife, then peel it. Use the knife to chop the crushed garlic finely.

Chopped ginger (top), chopped garlic (bottom)

SKINNING, DESEEDING & CHOPPING TOMATOES

1 Score crosses on the tops of the tomatoes. Place them in a pan of boiling water, leave for 30 seconds, then remove.

2 Pick up the split edges of the skin between your thumb and the blade of a sharp knife and peel off the skin.

3 Cut the tomatoes in half, and squeeze out all the seeds with your hands. Finely chop the tomato halves.

Skinned and deseeded tomato

COOKING METHODS

THE BASIC COOKING METHODS used in the recipes are explained here in detail, so use these pages as a reference guide in conjunction with the recipe section. The basic rules of each cooking method apply to whatever you are cooking. Follow them carefully to maximize the flavours and preserve the natural goodness of ingredients. Roasting and grilling foods help to seal in flavour; stir-frying retains the texture and nutrients; and sautéeing and braising moisten and add flavour to foods.

BASIC TECHNIQUES

STIR-FRYING

1 Assemble and prepare all the ingredients before you begin. Chop the ingredients in small, even-sized pieces, so that they cook quickly and evenly.

2 Heat a little oil in a wok and, when hot, add the ingredients one by one, according to the recipe, or beginning with those that will take longest to cook, such as onions and root vegetables.

3 Toss each ingredient vigorously for 1–2 minutes, before adding the next. Do not fill the wok more than one-third full, to ensure that all the ingredients cook properly.

SAUTEEING

Heat a little oil in a high-sided frying pan and cook ingredients over a medium to high heat, stirring, until golden.

BRAISING

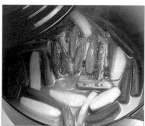

Carrots, celery, and other root vegetables are ideal for braising. Use a heavy pan with a lid, or a casserole. Put the prepared ingredients in the pan or casserole with enough stock, water, or wine to cover them. Bring to the boil, cover the pan tightly, and simmer over a low heat until the ingredients are just tender.

TOASTING SPICES

Toasting spices brings out their taste and aroma. A wok is ideal for this purpose, but if you do not have one, use a frying pan or any other pan with a heavy bottom.
Toss the spices vigorously over a high heat, in a dry pan, for 2–3 minutes until their aroma is released. Use as directed.

Crunchy stir-fried vegetables retain plenty of nutrients and taste

COOKING DRIED PULSES

All dried pulses, except lentils, need to be soaked overnight in water. After they have soaked, drain and rinse them, and place in a pan with twice their own volume of water. Always boil dried peas and beans rapidly for 10 minutes, then drain. Place in fresh water, bring to the boil, then simmer for the time shown.

COOKING TIMES FOR DRIED PULSES			
Aduki beans	45 minutes	Ful medames	2½–4 hours
Black beans	I–I½ hours	Haricot beans	I–I½ hours
Black-eye beans	I–I½ hours	Lentils	20–30 minutes
Borlotti beans	I–I½ hours	Mung beans	I hour
Butter beans	I–I½ hours	Pinto beans	I–I½ hours
Cannellini beans	I–I½ hours	Red kidney beans	I¾ hours
Chickpeas	2 hours	Soya beans	3½–4 hours
Flageolet beans	I–I½ hours	Split peas	2 hours

DEEP-FRYING

1 Fill a deep-fat fryer one-third full with oil. Heat the oil until hot. Drop a cube of bread into the fat. If it browns immediately, the oil is hot enough.

2 Fry the food in batches to prevent overcrowding. Cook according to the recipe. Drain on kitchen paper.

ROASTING VEGETABLES

Prepare the vegetables and cut them in large, even-sized chunks. Place in a roasting tray and drizzle with olive oil. Roast in a preheated oven at 230°C/450°F/Gas 8 for 40 minutes until golden and tender. Whole bulbs of garlic halved and roasted in this way have a delicious, sweet flavour.

GRILLING VEGETABLES

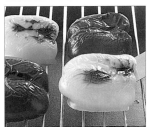

Prepare and trim the vegetables to be grilled, then halve them or cut them into thick slices. Brush them lightly with olive oil and grill under a hot, preheated grill, turning them at least once, until tender all the way through and slightly charred on all sides.

CHARGRILLING VEGETABLES

Heat a ridged griddle pan over a high heat. Prepare the vegetables in the same way as for grilling and place them on the hot griddle pan. Cook the vegetables over a high heat, turning them at least once, until tender and slightly charred on both sides.

Cooking vegetables on a ridged griddle pan creates attractive, charred stripes

PASTRY

ALTHOUGH FRESH PASTRY is now available in most supermarkets, preparing your own is well worth the effort. The key to good pastry is to work in a cool kitchen with cold ingredients and cold hands, and to handle the pastry as little as possible. All pastry doughs are enriched with fat. Some contain eggs, milk, or sugar, and can be flavoured according to taste with nuts, dried fruit, spices, herbs, or cheese. If you do not have time to make your own pastry, be sure to buy a brand that does not contain animal fat.

SHORTCRUST PASTRY

Makes 480g (1lb 1oz)

Shortcrust is the simplest pastry to make and can be used for most tarts and pies. Unless the recipe states otherwise, it is best cooked in a metal tin and baked blind before filling (see below, right) which keeps it crisp.

250g (9oz) plain flour, sifted, plus extra, to dust
175g (6oz) chilled, unsalted butter, cubed
1 egg, beaten
pinch salt

1 Place the flour in a bowl and add the butter. Rub the butter into the flour with your fingertips until the mixture resembles fine breadcrumbs.

2 Make a well in the centre and pour in the beaten egg. Add the pinch of salt.

3 Gently mix together with your fingertips to form a smooth dough.

4 Bring the dough together into a rough ball and wrap it in clingfilm. Leave in the refrigerator to rest for 30 minutes before use.

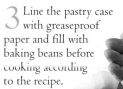

Clingfilm keeps dough moist

SWEET PASTRY

Makes 700g (1lb 9oz)

This pastry is ideal for making sweet tarts and pies.

325g (11½oz) plain flour, sifted, plus extra, to dust
225g (8oz) unsalted butter, at room temperature, cut in small pieces
pinch salt
100g (3½oz) icing sugar, sifted
finely grated zest of ½ lemon
1 egg, beaten

1 Place the flour in a bowl and make a well in the centre. Add the butter, salt, sugar, lemon zest, and egg.

2 Gradually mix in the flour with your fingertips until the ingredients come together to form a soft dough. Knead for 1 minute until smooth. Form into a ball, cover, and chill for 2 hours before use.

BAKING BLIND

1 Roll out the pastry and use the rolling pin to lift and transfer it into the tin.

2 Prick the pastry with a fork to prevent the pastry from rising up during baking.

3 Line the pastry case with greaseproof paper and fill with baking beans before cooking according to the recipe.

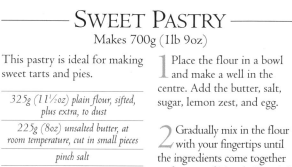

You can use ceramic or dried beans

PASTA

MAKING FRESH PASTA is easy. The dough can be mixed by hand on a clean work surface or made in a food processor. To use a food processor, put in the flour, salt, and olive oil, add the beaten eggs and egg yolk, and process until the mixture forms a dough. This takes a few seconds – it is important not to overwork the dough. Remove the dough from the food processor. If it is too dry, add a little water and knead in. If it is too wet, sprinkle with flour. Knead well, then cover and leave to rest.

— MAKING THE DOUGH —
Makes 375g (13oz)

It is best to handle this amount of ingredients on a clean work surface, but if you want to make half the quantity of dough, it may be easier to mix it in a bowl.

250g (9oz) strong plain flour, plus extra, to dust
pinch salt
2 large eggs, plus 1 large egg yolk
1 tbsp extra virgin olive oil
1 tbsp water

1 Sift the flour and salt on to a clean work surface, and form it into a mound. Make a well in the centre of the flour with your fingertips.

2 Put the eggs and egg yolk into the well in the flour, then add the oil and water. Gradually bring the flour into the centre with your fingertips.

3 Mix the flour into the eggs with your fingers until the ingredients are combined into a smooth paste. Gather the dough into a rough ball.

4 Knead the dough for 4–5 minutes until smooth and elastic. Cover in clingfilm and leave to rest for 30 minutes before rolling it out.

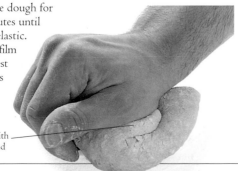

Knead dough with heel of your hand

— ROLLING & CUTTING —

A small, hand-operated pasta machine is the best tool for rolling out pasta dough. Not only does it roll out pasta accurately to the desired thickness, but it also helps to knead the dough. Pasta machines vary in size and price, but a basic model will do the job adequately. You will need to buy various cutting attachments to cut different shapes. If the dough sticks, dust it with a little flour.

1 Divide the dough into four. Sprinkle with flour on all sides, put the machine on the widest setting, then feed a piece of dough through the rollers.

2 Change the setting on the machine by one notch. Fold the pasta in half, and dust with flour, then feed it through the rollers once again.

3 Repeat the process four or five times, decreasing the space between the rollers each time, until the pasta reaches the desired thickness.

4 Lay the pasta sheets on tea towels to dry for 5–10 minutes. Attach the relevant cutter to the machine and feed the pasta through. For lasagne and cannelloni cut by hand.

Guide pasta sheet through rollers with your hand

BASIC RECIPES

STOCKS ARE NOT as time-consuming to make as is often believed. Simply let the stock bubble away while you prepare the recipe. The recipes in this book call for specific stocks. Some recipes require a delicately flavoured vegetable stock, while others require the deeper flavour of a mushroom stock. Always use fresh, good quality ingredients for the most nutritious and flavoursome results.

STOCKS & SAUCES

VEGETABLE STOCK

Makes 1 litre (1¾ pints)

2 tbsp extra virgin olive oil

1 onion, roughly chopped

1 small leek, roughly chopped

75g (2¾oz) celeriac, roughly chopped

2 large carrots, roughly chopped

1 celery stick, roughly chopped

75g (2¾oz) white cabbage, roughly chopped

½ fennel, roughly chopped

4 garlic cloves, chopped

125ml (4fl oz) white wine, optional

4 black peppercorns

1 sprig thyme

1 small bay leaf

2 tsp sea salt

1 Heat the olive oil in a large pan, add all the vegetables and garlic, and cook over a low heat for about 5 minutes.

2 Pour in the wine, if using, then add the peppercorns, thyme, bay leaf, and 1.4 litres (2½ pints) water. Bring to the boil, add the sea salt, and skim off any scum. Reduce the heat to very low and simmer the stock gently for 40 minutes until reduced by one-third of its original volume.

3 Strain the stock through a fine sieve and leave to cool. Cover and keep in the refrigerator until required, but for a maximum of 1 week.

DARK VEGETABLE STOCK

Makes 1 litre (1¾ pints)

4 tbsp vegetable oil

½ onion, roughly chopped

2 large carrots, roughly chopped

1 leek, roughly chopped

1 celery stick, roughly chopped

2 garlic cloves, chopped

100g (3½oz) flat mushrooms, roughly chopped

2 ripe beef tomatoes, roughly chopped

2 sprigs thyme

few parsley stalks

1 bay leaf

1 heaped tsp granulated sugar

½ tbsp sea salt

2 tbsp dark soy sauce

1 Heat the vegetable oil in a large pan, add the onion, carrots, leek, celery, and garlic, and sauté over a medium heat for about 5 minutes until lightly coloured.

2 Add the mushrooms and sauté for 5 minutes over a low heat until golden. Add the tomatoes, herbs, and sugar and cook for a further 5 minutes. Stir in 1.4 litres (2½ pints) water. Bring to the boil, add the sea salt, and skim off any scum. Simmer the stock gently for 45 minutes.

3 Stir in the soy sauce, strain through a fine sieve, and cool. Cover and keep in the refrigerator (see left).

BROWN MUSHROOM STOCK

Makes 1 litre (1¾ pints)

100g (3½oz) unsalted butter

3 shallots, finely diced

2 garlic cloves, sliced

200g (7oz) button mushrooms

600g (1lb 5oz) flat mushrooms, roughly chopped

1 tbsp tomato purée

4 ripe tomatoes, roughly chopped

few parsley stalks

4 tbsp tamari

1 Melt the butter, add the shallots and garlic, and sweat them over a medium heat until softened.

2 Add the mushrooms and cook, stirring, until they are deep brown and lightly caramelized. Stir in the tomato purée and tomatoes, and simmer for 10 minutes.

3 Pour in 1.7 litres (3 pints) water, add the parsley stalks, and bring to the boil. Skim any scum off the surface of the stock with a slotted spoon, then reduce the heat and simmer for 25 minutes. Stir in the tamari and remove from the heat.

4 Strain the stock through a fine sieve and leave until completely cool. Cover and keep in the refrigerator until required (see left).

MADEIRA SAUCE

Makes 600ml (1 pint)

4 tbsp vegetable oil

½ onion, roughly chopped

2 large carrots, chopped

1 leek, chopped

1 celery stick, chopped

2 garlic cloves, chopped

100g (3½oz) flat mushrooms, chopped

2 large tomatoes, chopped

2 sprigs thyme

1 bay leaf

1 tsp caster sugar

1 tsp salt

25g (1oz) unsalted butter

25g (1oz) porcini, soaked in water, drained, and chopped

2 tbsp Madeira

1 Heat the oil, add the onion, carrots, leek, celery, and garlic, and sauté over a medium heat for 5 minutes. Add the flat mushrooms and cook for a further 5 minutes.

2 Stir in the tomatoes, herbs, and sugar, and simmer gently for 5 minutes. Add 850ml (1½ pints) water, bring to the boil, then add the salt. Simmer for 45 minutes. Strain through a fine sieve.

3 Heat the butter and fry the porcini for 2 minutes over a low heat. Pour in the Madeira and stock. Simmer until reduced by half. Season.

OTHER USEFUL RECIPES

ROASTED CHERRY TOMATO SALSA

Serves 4

250g (9oz) cherry tomatoes, halved

1 garlic clove, crushed

4 tbsp olive oil

1 tbsp chopped fresh basil

good pinch caster sugar

2 tbsp lime or lemon juice

salt and freshly ground pepper

Preheat the oven to 240°C/ 475°F/Gas 9. Place the cherry tomatoes and garlic in a roasting tin. Sprinkle with the basil and sugar, then drizzle with 2 tablespoons of olive oil. Season, then bake for 2–3 minutes until the tomatoes are just tender. Transfer the tomatoes to a large bowl. Add the lime juice and remaining olive oil and toss together gently to mix. Serve warm or cold.

FRESH TOMATO SAUCE

Makes 300ml (½ pint)

6 tbsp olive oil

½ onion, roughly chopped

2 garlic cloves, crushed

sprig fresh thyme

750g (1lb 10oz) ripe tomatoes

1 tbsp tomato purée

pinch caster sugar

425ml (¾ pint) Vegetable Stock (see opposite)

salt and freshly ground pepper

Heat the olive oil in a pan, add the onion, garlic, and thyme, and sweat over a medium heat until soft. Roughly chop the tomatoes and add to the pan with the tomato purée and sugar. Season, then add the vegetable stock. Bring to the boil. Reduce the heat and simmer for 10–15 minutes until the tomatoes are reduced to a pulp. Strain the sauce through a fine sieve to serve.

LEMON PEPPER

Preheat the oven to 160°C/ 325°F/Gas 3. Peel 4 lemons with a potato peeler. Spread the peel out on a clean baking sheet and bake for 1 hour until the skins are dried and shrivelled. Leave to cool. When cool, place the peel in a coffee grinder, in small batches, and grind to a fine powder. Store the lemon pepper in an airtight container for up to 1 month.

VINAIGRETTE

Makes 200ml (7fl oz)

3 tbsp quality red wine vinegar

1–1½ tbsp Dijon mustard

1 small garlic clove, crushed

5 tbsp extra virgin olive oil

5 tbsp groundnut or vegetable oil

salt and freshly ground pepper

Mix the vinegar, mustard, and garlic in a bowl. Pour in the oils and whisk. Season.

OLIVADA

Makes 150g (5½oz)

125g (4½oz) pitted black olives, finely chopped

2 garlic cloves

4 tbsp olive oil

salt and freshly ground pepper

Blend all the ingredients to a coarse purée in a blender or food processor. Transfer to a bowl, cover, and store in the refrigerator for up to 4 days.

LABNA

Makes 125g (4½oz)

Line a colander with four layers of dampened muslin. Pour 250g/9oz yogurt into the muslin, gather together the edges of the muslin, tie them, and suspend over a bowl. Leave to drain in a cool place for 3–4 days, or a minimum of 1 day. When the milky liquid has drained off it will leave a thick-textured, creamy yogurt.

RECIPES

This collection of recipes will change the way you

think about vegetarian cookery. The dishes

make use of the array of produce and flavourings that

is available to us from around the world,

to produce a new generation of vegetarian cuisine.

Classic recipes are given new interpretations,

and novel and exciting combinations of ingredients

are used for maximum impact.

STARTERS & FINGER FOOD

THESE RECIPES DRAW influences from every corner of the globe, including South America, the Mediterranean, the Middle East, and the Orient. Their wonderful flavours and textures range from simple and rustic to elegant and refined: there is something to suit every occasion. Although the recipes in this chapter are specifically designed to whet the appetite, and will provide an impressive prelude to any meal, they also make delicious light meals suitable for serving as main courses.

LAYERED MEDITERRANEAN GATEAU WITH LABNA

KEY INGREDIENTS

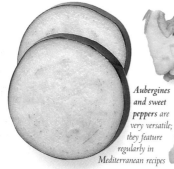

Basil is highly aromatic and gives a wonderful flavour to many Mediterranean dishes

Labna is an easy-to-make strained yogurt

Aubergines and sweet peppers are very versatile; they feature regularly in Mediterranean recipes

Coriander is useful as a garnish or in cooking

Tomatoes are delicious served simply

Our passion for the light, fresh, healthy cooking of the Mediterranean continues to grow and grow. This layered savoury gâteau is not only visually stunning, but also bursting with flavour. Labna is a strained yogurt that is easy to make and well worth the effort. If you do not have a ring mould just carefully build the layers of vegetables on the baking sheet.

INGREDIENTS

200ml (7fl oz) olive oil, plus oil, to grease

1 aubergine, cut in 5mm (¼ inch) slices

handful fresh basil leaves

1 garlic clove

4 peppers (2 red, 1 yellow, 1 green) roasted, peeled, deseeded (see page 39), and quartered

4 plum tomatoes, cut in thick slices

4 tbsp Labna (see page 45)

sprig fresh basil, to garnish

FOR THE VINAIGRETTE

2 tbsp chopped fresh basil or coriander

2 tbsp red wine vinegar

6 tbsp olive oil

1 tomato, skinned, deseeded, and chopped (see page 39)

salt and freshly ground pepper

1 Heat 150ml (¼ pint) of the olive oil in a heavy-bottomed frying pan. Fry the aubergine for 5 minutes on each side over a medium heat until golden. Drain.

2 In a blender or food processor, purée together the basil and garlic with 2 tablespoons of olive oil. Place four 7cm (2¾ inch) metal ring moulds on a lightly greased baking sheet.

3 Layer the vegetables in the moulds: start with a slice of aubergine, then continue with 1 teaspoon of basil purée, alternate pieces of the red, yellow, and green pepper, more basil purée, another slice of aubergine, then basil purée again. Top with a layer of tomatoes.

4 Press down lightly, drizzle with the remaining olive oil, then bake for 10 minutes. Place the moulds on serving plates, then carefully lift off the moulds. Blend together all the ingredients for the vinaigrette. To serve, garnish each gâteau with a spoonful of labna, a drizzle of vinaigrette, and a sprig of basil.

Oven preheated to 180°C/350°F/Gas 4

Preparation & cooking time 50 minutes

Serves 4

Nutritional notes
kcalories 693; protein 5g; carbohydrate 14g; total fat 69g, of which saturated fat 10g; fibre 4g; sodium 145mg

GOAT'S CHEESE LATKES WITH BEETROOT SALSA

This sumptuous version of the famous Jewish potato pancakes includes courgettes, which provide both colour and flavour, and a rich, tangy goat's cheese filling. The salsa is a modern interpretation of classical Eastern European flavours.

INGREDIENTS

450g (1lb) starchy potatoes, peeled
1 medium courgette
1 large onion
1 egg yolk, beaten
3 tbsp arrowroot or potato flour
vegetable oil, for frying
4 crottin de chavignol or other firm goat's cheeses, about 75g (2¾oz) each
salt and freshly ground pepper
soured cream, to serve
fresh basil leaves, to garnish

FOR THE SALSA

2 medium beetroots, boiled and diced
2 shallots, chopped
¼ tsp caraway seeds
2 tbsp red wine vinegar
2 tbsp olive oil
2 tbsp chopped fresh basil
1 red chilli, deseeded and chopped
1 tbsp maple syrup or honey

1 For the salsa, place the diced beetroot in a bowl and add the remaining ingredients. Season, then stir to combine. Cover and leave for the flavours to infuse for about 2 hours.

2 Grate the potatoes, courgette, and onion on the largest holes of the grater, then put them in a clean tea towel and squeeze out any excess moisture. Transfer to a bowl, season, and stir in the egg yolk until thoroughly mixed. Sift in the arrowroot and beat vigorously until well combined.

3 Heat the oil in a frying pan. Dip the cheeses in the batter to coat them, then place, well spaced out, in the pan. Fry over a medium heat for 2–3 minutes on either side until golden, then drain on kitchen paper. Serve with soured cream and a good spoonful of salsa, and garnish with basil leaves.

Preparation & cooking time
1 hour, plus 2 hours infusing time

Serves 4

Nutritional notes
kcalories 684; protein 27g; carbohydrate 55g; total fat 41g, of which saturated fat 21g; fibre 3g; sodium 645mg

CAPONATA ON ROASTED GARLIC BRUSCHETTA

Caponata, a sweet-and-sour stew from Sicily, makes a wonderful topping for bruschetta. Roasting the garlic gives a mellow sweetness that contrasts well with the piquancy of the vegetables.

INGREDIENTS

½ medium aubergine
3 peppers (1 red, 1 yellow, 1 green), deseeded
1 courgette
2 celery sticks
1 red onion, sliced
2 tbsp honey
2 tbsp balsamic vinegar
1 tbsp raisins, soaked overnight in water
1 tbsp pine kernels, toasted
salt and freshly ground pepper

FOR THE BRUSCHETTA

3 whole garlic cloves, unpeeled
5 tbsp olive oil
8 thick slices Italian bread
thin shavings Parmesan
basil and rocket leaves, to garnish

1 In a small, ovenproof dish, toss the garlic in 1 tablespoon of olive oil and roast for 30 minutes until soft and caramelized; set aside.

2 Cut the vegetables into 1cm (½ inch) pieces. In a pan, heat 2 tablespoons of olive oil and sauté the onion for 5 minutes over a medium heat until golden. Add the remaining vegetables and cook over a low heat for about 10 minutes until tender. Stir in the remaining ingredients; season.

3 Brush the bread slices with the remaining oil and bake for 10 minutes until golden. Squeeze the roasted garlic out of its skin and spread over the toast, then pile on the vegetables. Top with Parmesan, basil, and rocket.

Oven preheated to
200°C/400°F/Gas 6

Preparation & cooking time
1 hour, plus overnight soaking time

Serves 4

Nutritional notes
kcalories 557; protein 16g; carbohydrate 81g; total fat 21g, of which saturated fat 3g; fibre 9g; sodium 1708mg

GRILLED ASPARAGUS WITH GREMOLATA

Asparagus is usually served steamed, but I find that it has a much better flavour when grilled because the direct contact with the heat caramelizes it slightly. Choose very fresh, brightly coloured stems – if they are at all withered they will be tough and bitter to taste.

INGREDIENTS

finely grated zest of 1 lemon

2 tbsp chopped fresh flatleaf parsley

1 tbsp chopped fresh basil

150ml (¼ pint) Vinaigrette (see page 45)

32 fat asparagus stalks, trimmed

6 tbsp olive oil

salt and freshly ground pepper

FOR THE GREMOLATA

3 slices white bread, crusts removed

50g (1¾oz) butter, melted

1 For the gremolata, process the bread to a coarse, crumb-like texture in a blender or food processor, then mix in the butter. Spread on a baking sheet, then bake for 15 minutes until golden.

2 Meanwhile, mix the lemon zest and chopped herbs into the vinaigrette. Put the asparagus on to wooden skewers that have been soaked in water (about six per skewer), so that they lie across the skewers (this makes it easier to turn them). Place in a dish, pour the olive oil over them, season, and leave for 5–10 minutes to allow the salt to tenderize them slightly.

3 Grill the asparagus on a heated grill pan or under a hot grill for 4 minutes until tender, turning them occasionally.

4 To serve, remove the skewers and place the asparagus on a large serving plate. Drizzle with the vinaigrette, then scatter the gremolata over the top.

Oven preheated to 190°C/375°F/Gas 5

Preparation & cooking time 1 hour

Serves 4

Nutritional notes kcalories 480; protein 9g; carbohydrate 16g; total fat 43g, of which saturated fat 11g; fibre 4g; sodium 295mg

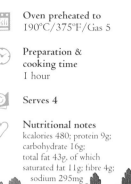

SAVOURY ROQUEFORT MOUSSE

These delicious mousses are simple and quick to make. The sauce can be prepared in advance, one or two hours before needed, but do not put it in the refrigerator, because this will spoil the texture.

INGREDIENTS

300ml (½ pint) milk

50g (1¾oz) unsalted butter, plus extra, to grease

50g (1¾oz) plain flour

3 eggs, plus 2 egg yolks

250ml (9fl oz) single cream

50g (1¾oz) cream cheese

75g (2¾oz) Roquefort, mashed

salt and freshly ground pepper

pinch ground nutmeg

FOR THE ROASTED PEPPER SAUCE

2 large red peppers, roasted, peeled, deseeded (see page 39), and chopped

300ml (½ pint) Vegetable Stock (see page 44)

2 tbsp olive oil

1 For the roasted pepper sauce, place the peppers in a blender or food processor with the stock, olive oil, and seasoning. Blend to a smooth paste.

2 In a small pan, bring the milk and butter to the boil. Sift in the flour and beat well until the mixture thickens. Reduce the heat to low and continue to cook for 2 minutes, beating continuously.

3 Add the eggs, egg yolks, and cream to the pan, beating to form a thick sauce. Stir in the cream cheese, Roquefort, salt, pepper, and nutmeg.

4 Butter four individual ramekins and fill with the cheese mixture. Place the ramekins in a roasting tin, then pour in enough boiling water to come one-third of the way up the sides.

5 Bake for 15–20 minutes until lightly set and golden. Turn the mousses out on to serving plates. To serve, heat the roasted pepper sauce and pour a little sauce around each mousse.

Oven preheated to 160°C/325°F/Gas 3

Preparation & cooking time 1¼ hours, plus 1 hour for the stock

Serves 4

Nutritional notes kcalories 392; protein 14g; carbohydrate 10g; total fat 33g, of which saturated fat 16g; fibre 2g; sodium 527mg

WOK & ROLL

These delightful, tiny spring rolls have a classic elegance that I associate with Chinese cuisine. They are light and crispy on the outside and moist and delicately spicy on the inside. Ready-to-use spring-roll wrappers are now more widely available in supermarkets than they were in the past. The beauty of these spring rolls is that they can be prepared in advance up to the end of step three and frozen for up to three months. Serve with Chinese Dipping Sauce (see below).

INGREDIENTS

12 spring-roll wrappers, each about 20cm (8 inches) square

1 egg, beaten

vegetable oil, for deep-frying

1 tbsp black or toasted sesame seeds

Chinese Dipping Sauce (see below), to serve

FOR THE STIR-FRY

4 tbsp vegetable oil

1 garlic clove, crushed

4cm (1½ inch) piece fresh root ginger, chopped

½ green pepper, cored, deseeded, and cut in julienne strips

1 celery stick, thinly sliced

1 carrot, cut in julienne strips

50g (1¾oz) Chinese cabbage, shredded

2 tbsp hoisin sauce

salt and freshly ground pepper

FOR THE SLAW

¼ cucumber, shredded

50g (1¾oz) beansprouts

1 small red chilli, deseeded and thinly sliced

4 tbsp rice wine vinegar

4 tbsp light soy sauce

2 tbsp maple syrup

1 For the stir-fry, heat a wok over a high heat until it is very hot, then add the oil. Fry the garlic and ginger for a few seconds to flavour the oil, then stir-fry the vegetables: add the green pepper first and stir-fry for 1 minute, then add the celery and fry for a further minute. Next add the carrot and Chinese cabbage. Continue cooking for 1 minute more, then season. Place in a bowl to cool, then refrigerate.

2 For the slaw, put the shredded cucumber, beansprouts, and red chilli in a bowl. Blend together the rice wine vinegar, soy sauce, and maple syrup, then mix into the slaw. Cover and set aside. Mix the hoisin sauce in with the stir-fried vegetables; adjust the seasoning.

3 Lay the spring-roll wrappers on a work surface and brush with beaten egg. Put 1 tablespoon of the stir-fry in the centre of each wrapper, fold the edges in a little, then roll the wrapper up tightly into a cigar shape. Seal the edges with beaten egg.

4 Heat the oil in the wok. Deep-fry the rolls, a few at a time, for 3 minutes until golden. Drain. Place a portion of slaw on each plate and lay two spring rolls on top. Scatter with the sesame seeds. Serve with dipping sauce.

Preparation & cooking time
40 minutes, plus 1 hour for the dipping sauce

Serves 4

Nutritional notes
kcalories 459; protein 9g; carbohydrate 38g; total fat 31g, of which saturated fat 4g; fibre 2g; sodium 1617mg

CHINESE DIPPING SAUCE

Dipping sauces form an integral part of Chinese cooking, and this sauce is one of my particular favourites. I often use it as a base for a salad dressing, add it to stir-fries, or serve it with Wok & Roll (see above).

INGREDIENTS

1 tbsp light soy sauce

2 shallots, finely chopped

2 tbsp rice wine vinegar

2 tsp sesame oil

½ tbsp caster sugar

1cm (½ inch) piece fresh root ginger, finely grated

½ small red chilli, deseeded and finely chopped

1 Mix together all the sauce ingredients in a bowl and stir until well combined. Cover and leave to chill in the refrigerator, to allow the flavours to infuse, for at least 1 hour before serving. Serves four.

GREQUE OF VEGETABLES WITH HERB CHEESE

Although this recipe is not an authentically Greek one, it captures some typical flavours and textures. The herb cheese is simple to make and versatile; it spreads well for sandwiches and makes a wonderful dip. Basil, parsley, and tarragon make a good herb mix for flavouring the cheese. Chanterelles are best for this recipe, but if they are not available you can replace them with button mushrooms. Serve the dish with warm pitta bread.

INGREDIENTS

6 tbsp olive oil

250g (9oz) baby courgettes, halved lengthways

12 spring onions, trimmed

250g (9oz) chanterelles

1 garlic clove, crushed

juice of 2 lemons

1 tsp coriander seeds

1 bay leaf

leaves from sprig fresh thyme

150ml (¼ pint) dry white wine

lightly cracked black peppercorns

chives, to garnish

FOR THE HERB CHEESE

150g (5½oz) feta

100g (3½oz) cream cheese

1 garlic clove, crushed

1 tbsp chopped mixed fresh herbs

4 tbsp double cream

pinch cayenne pepper

salt and freshly ground pepper

1 Heat the oil in a frying pan. Sauté the courgettes, onions and chanterelles over a medium to high heat for 2–3 minutes. Reduce the heat to medium and add the remaining ingredients. Cook, stirring, for a further 8–10 minutes. When the vegetables are just tender, but not too soft, remove from the heat and leave to cool.

2 For the herb cheese, blend together the feta, cream cheese, and garlic in a blender or food processor. Add the mixed herbs, then blend again. Stir in the cream and cayenne pepper, and season. Form the herb cheese into eight oval quenelles, using two dessert spoons.

3 Divide the vegetables between four plates. Place two herb cheese quenelles on each plate and garnish with chives, then serve.

Preparation & cooking time
50 minutes

Serves 4

Nutritional notes
kcalories 534; protein 10g; carbohydrate 4g; total fat 51g, of which saturated fat 24g; fibre 1g; sodium 733mg

STACKED VEGETABLE CEVICHE

Ceviche is a South American dish of thinly sliced raw fish "cooked" in a chilli-spiced, citrus marinade. I have used the same flavourings in this dressing for crunchy raw vegetables, layered between crispy corn tortillas, for a very special starter.

INGREDIENTS

1 medium cauliflower, cut in small florets

2 tomatoes, skinned, deseeded, and chopped (see page 39)

50g (1¾ oz) cucumber, peeled and diced

1 small green apple, peeled and diced

2 Carmel avocados (smooth-skinned), diced and sprinkled with lemon juice

4 radicchio, shredded

4 spring onions, shredded

8 corn tortillas, deep-fried until crisp

mizuna leaves, to garnish

FOR THE DRESSING

1 red chilli

juice of 2 limes

zest and juice of 1 orange

1 tbsp coriander seeds, crushed

½ tsp caster sugar

1 garlic clove, crushed

2 tbsp soured cream

2 tbsp chopped fresh coriander

1 For the dressing, roast the chilli for 15 minutes then, when cool enough to handle, cut in half, remove the seeds, and chop the chilli finely. Place in a bowl and toss together with the remaining ingredients. Cover, and set aside to marinate for about 4 hours.

2 Blanch the cauliflower florets in boiling, salted water for 2 minutes. Refresh in cold water, drain, and place in a clean bowl. Add the tomatoes, cucumber, apple, avocados, radicchio, and spring onions.

3 Pour the dressing over the vegetables. Cover with clingfilm and leave to marinate in the refrigerator for a further 30 minutes. Serve chilled, layering the vegetables between the crispy fried tortillas (serving two tortillas per person). Garnish each one with a mizuna leaf.

Oven preheated to
220°C/425°F/Gas 7

Preparation & cooking time
30 minutes, plus 4 hours marinating time

Serves 4

Nutritional notes
kcalories 402; protein 14g; carbohydrate 80g; total fat 6g, of which saturated fat 2g; fibre 7g; sodium 333mg

MINTED ASPARAGUS TARTLETS

Filled with a purée of asparagus and fromage frais, these tartlets are deliciously light. I love the combination of asparagus and mint — perfect for an early summer meal. Alternatively, you could use other herbs, such as basil, parsley, or chervil.

INGREDIENTS

250g (9oz) Shortcrust Pastry (see page 42)

400g (14oz) asparagus, trimmed

100g (3½oz) fromage frais

25g (1oz) butter, plus extra, to grease

1 onion, chopped

1 garlic clove, crushed

2 tbsp chopped fresh mint

25g (1oz) plain flour

salt and freshly ground pepper

1 Grease four 7cm (2¾ inch) tart tins. Roll out the pastry on a floured surface and use to line the tart tins. Cover with greaseproof paper and baking beans, and bake blind for 5–6 minutes. Remove the paper and beans, and bake for a further 3–4 minutes; leave to cool.

2 Steam the asparagus for 2–3 minutes until just tender. Drain and refresh in cold water. Trim off the tips and reserve them. Place the stems in a blender or food processor with the fromage frais; blend until smooth.

3 Melt the butter in a small pan, add the onion, garlic, and mint, and sauté over a low heat for 2 minutes until softened. Sift in the flour, stir well, and cook for a further 2 minutes. Stir in the asparagus purée, then whisk over a low heat until the sauce is thick. Season to taste.

4 Pour the sauce into the pastry cases, arrange the asparagus tips on top, and bake for a further 5 minutes. Serve hot or cold.

Oven preheated to
190°C/375°F/Gas 5

Preparation & cooking time
35 minutes, plus 40 minutes for the pastry

Serves 4

Nutritional notes
kcalories 418; protein 10g; carbohydrate 36g; total fat 27g, of which saturated fat 17g; fibre 3g; sodium 123mg

BLACK BEAN FALAFEL

Falafel are virtually Israel's national dish. These little chickpea fritters are usually eaten stuffed into warm pitta bread and served with a tahini dressing. Here they are presented elegantly on a bed of salad with baked red onions and crisp spinach (see Red Onion Salad with Tahini Dressing, below).

INGREDIENTS

4 slices white bread, crusts removed

450g (1lb) chickpeas, soaked in cold water for 24 hours

25g (1oz) plain flour or chickpea flour

225g (8oz) onion, roughly chopped

2 tbsp chopped fresh parsley

2 tbsp chopped fresh coriander

2 large garlic cloves, crushed

1 tsp cayenne pepper

1 tsp ground cumin

200g (7oz) dried black beans, soaked overnight, cooked (see page 41), and drained

vegetable oil, for frying

Red Onion Salad with Tahini Dressing (see below), to serve

1 Place the bread in a bowl. Pour 150ml (¼ pint) of cold water over the bread. Leave to soak for 10 minutes.

2 Drain the chickpeas and mince to a fine pulp in a blender or food processor. Transfer to a bowl with the flour.

3 Mince the onion, parsley, and coriander in a blender or food processor, then add the garlic, cayenne pepper, and cumin. Blend again, then mix with the chickpeas and flour.

4 Squeeze the excess water from the bread with your hands and add to the mixture. Work all the ingredients together until well blended, then stir in the cooked black beans and mix until thoroughly incorporated.

5 Shape into small cakes, approximately 5cm (2 inches) in diameter and 2cm (¾ inch) thick. Leave to rest in the refrigerator for 30 minutes until the mixture has firmed up.

6 Heat the oil in a large frying pan and shallow-fry the falafel for 3–4 minutes on each side over a medium heat until golden. Drain the excess oil on kitchen paper. Serve on a bed of the red onion salad with tahini dressing.

Preparation & cooking time
2½ hours, plus 24 hours soaking time

Serves 4

Nutritional notes
kcalories 878; protein 26g; carbohydrate 68g; total fat 58g, of which saturated fat 8g; fibre 12g; sodium 138mg

RED ONION SALAD WITH TAHINI DRESSING

The inclusion of mustard in the tahini dressing is unusual, but it gives a nice bite. The onions have a wonderfully sweet and tangy flavour when mixed with the dressing and baked. Serve with the Black Bean Falafel (see above).

INGREDIENTS

FOR THE SALAD

2 red onions

300g (10½oz) young spinach

FOR THE TAHINI DRESSING

6 tbsp water

3 tbsp white wine vinegar

3 tbsp tahini

2 tbsp coarse-grain mustard

1 tbsp honey

1 garlic clove, crushed

125ml (4fl oz) olive oil

1 For the dressing, whisk together all the ingredients in a bowl until smooth.

2 Peel the onions without removing the roots, then cut the onions into separate wedges (the root holds the wedges intact). Place in a baking dish and cover with half the dressing. Leave to marinate for 2 hours, then bake for 30 minutes until tender.

3 Place the spinach in a bowl, add the onions, and the remaining dressing, reserving just a little to serve. Toss until the salad is well coated.

4 Divide the onion salad equally between four serving plates, and drizzle with the remaining dressing.

Oven preheated to
200°C/400°F/Gas 6

Preparation & cooking time
55 minutes, plus 2 hours marinating time

Serves 4

Nutritional notes
kcalories 455; protein 7g; carbohydrate 15g; total fat 41g, of which saturated fat 6g; fibre 5g; sodium 226mg

ORIENTAL MUSHROOM SUSHI PURSES

With a surprise filling of shiitake mushrooms spiced with searingly hot Japanese horseradish, these little pastry purses taste as good as they look. They can be assembled in advance and cooked just before serving. Serve with a bowl of soy or plum sauce for dipping.

INGREDIENTS

150g (5½oz) sushi or short-grain rice
½ tsp granulated sugar
50ml (2fl oz) rice wine vinegar
2 tbsp sesame oil
1 garlic clove, crushed
75g (2¾oz) shiitake mushrooms, sliced
¼ tsp wasabi (Japanese horseradish)
2 spring onions, shredded
1 tbsp soy sauce
20 spring-roll or wonton wrappers
1 egg, beaten
1 tbsp black or toasted sesame seeds
vegetable oil, for deep-frying
salt and freshly ground pepper

1 Boil the rice for 20 minutes according to packet instructions until tender. Remove from the heat and leave to stand, covered, for 10 minutes.

2 Place the sugar and vinegar in a large pan and warm them together over a low heat, stirring until the sugar has dissolved. Stir in the hot rice and leave to cool.

3 Heat the sesame oil and sauté the garlic and mushrooms over a medium heat for 2–3 minutes. Place in a bowl with the wasabi, spring onions, and soy sauce, then season.

4 To assemble, dampen your hands with water and roll the rice into 2.5cm (1 inch) balls. Make a small hole in the centre of each rice ball with your thumb. Spoon a little of the mushroom and onion filling into the hole. Close up the rice around the filling. Repeat until all the mixture is used.

5 Lay the spring-roll wrappers on a clean work surface and brush them liberally with the beaten egg. Place a rice ball on each wrapper, then draw up the corners of the wrapper to form a small purse. Push the neck together to seal in the rice ball.

6 Brush with beaten egg, then sprinkle with sesame seeds. Deep-fry a few at a time in hot oil for 2–3 minutes or bake for 10–12 minutes until golden.

Oven preheated to 190°C/375°F/Gas 5

Preparation & cooking time 1–1¼ hours

Makes 20

Nutritional notes kcalories 128; protein 4g; carbohydrate 11g; total fat 8g, of which saturated fat 1g; fibre 0.1g; sodium 71mg

CHILLI-MARINATED OLIVES

Marinating is an easy way of livening up plain olives. Try adding herbs or some finely grated lemon zest for interesting variations.

INGREDIENTS

150g (5½ oz) pitted green olives
100g (3½ oz) pitted black olives
4 tomatoes, skinned, deseeded, and finely chopped (see page 39)
120ml (3¾ fl oz) vegetable oil
2 garlic cloves, crushed
1 tbsp tomato purée
1 tsp dried chilli flakes

1 In a small pan, cover the olives with cold water and bring to the boil. Drain the olives, rinse under cold water for a few seconds, then place back in the pan and cover with water again. Bring to the boil once more, then drain again and set aside.

2 Place all the remaining ingredients in a separate pan and simmer on a low heat for 8–10 minutes. Add the olives, with 150ml (¼ pint) water, and simmer over a low heat until the water has been absorbed. Leave to cool, preferably overnight, but for at least a few hours.

3 To serve, spear the olives with cocktail sticks, which can be picked up by hand.

Preparation & cooking time 35 minutes, plus at least 4 hours cooling time

Serves 10

Nutritional notes kcalories 141; protein 0.6g; carbohydrate 1.3g; total fat 15g, of which saturated fat 2g; fibre 1g; sodium 573mg

GUACAMOLE & CHEESE CHALUPAS

In Mexico, fried tortillas form the basis of an endless variety of snacks. They are often served piled high with wonderful contrasting ingredients and called "chalupas" (which means little boats). This version is topped with tangy guacamole mixed with goat's cheese.

INGREDIENTS

vegetable oil, for deep-frying
4 corn tortillas, 12cm (4½ inches) each, quartered
1 large avocado
125g (4½oz) firm goat's cheese, grated
½ red onion, diced
1 tsp cumin seeds
3 tsp lemon juice
Tabasco, to taste
salt and freshly ground pepper
6 tbsp natural yogurt, to serve
1 tbsp chopped fresh coriander, to garnish

1 Heat the oil in a large frying pan or deep-fat fryer. When hot, deep-fry the tortillas for 2 minutes until crisp and golden. Alternatively, you can bake the tortillas for 20 minutes.

2 Mash together the avocado and goat's cheese. Add the onion, cumin seeds, lemon juice, Tabasco, and seasoning.

3 Top each tortilla with the guacamole, then a little yogurt. Sprinkle the coriander on top, to garnish.

Oven preheated to 180°C/350°F/Gas 4

Preparation & cooking time
20–25 minutes

Makes 24

Nutritional notes
kcalories 90; protein 3g; carbohydrate 7g; total fat 6g, of which saturated fat 2g; fibre 0.6g; sodium 91mg

EGG MAYO & WATERCRESS CROUTES

Egg mayonnaise and watercress is a great sandwich filling, which we probably all take for granted, but serving it warm on toasted baguettes gives a new twist to this classic combination.

INGREDIENTS

5 hard-boiled eggs, finely chopped
1 bunch spring onions, finely chopped
1 small bunch watercress, finely chopped
4 tbsp good-quality mayonnaise
2 tbsp freshly grated Parmesan
4 mini baguettes, sliced and toasted
salt and freshly ground pepper

1 Place the hard-boiled eggs in a medium bowl and mix in the remaining ingredients. Season to taste and chill until needed.

2 Spoon the egg mixture on to the toasts. Grill until golden.

VARIATION

Brie & Mushroom Croûtes
Heat 1 tablespoon olive oil and sauté 2 crushed garlic cloves with ½ teaspoon fresh thyme leaves until soft. Add 200g (7oz) chopped mushrooms and cook over a high heat for 8–10 minutes. Stir in 1 tablespoon balsamic vinegar; simmer for 2 minutes. Top each toast with a slice of Brie and the mushrooms; grill as above.

Preparation & cooking time
15 minutes

Makes 24

Nutritional notes
kcalories 119; protein 4g; carbohydrate 11g; total fat 7g, of which saturated fat 1g; fibre 0.4g; sodium 177mg

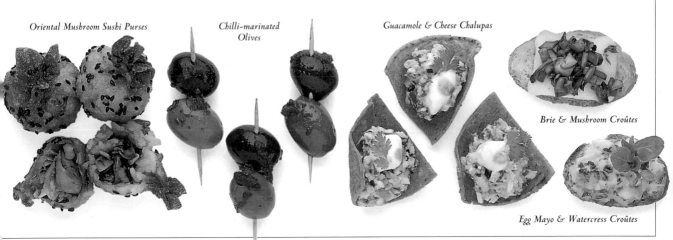

Oriental Mushroom Sushi Purses

Chilli-marinated Olives

Guacamole & Cheese Chalupas

Brie & Mushroom Croûtes

Egg Mayo & Watercress Croûtes

SOUPS

SOUP HAS BEEN A POPULAR DISH throughout the ages. It can be made from any vegetable, enhanced with exotic spices and other flavourings, fresh herbs, grains, and pulses. Soup is a comforting food in winter; a thick broth needs little more than a hunk of crusty bread to accompany it. For warmer days there are lighter and more delicate consommés: soups that can be served hot and some that can be served chilled. Here you will see how versatile soups can be, and how quick and easy they are to prepare.

LAZY CARIBBEAN SOUP

KEY INGREDIENTS

Passion fruit has an intense flavour and a lovely sweetness: the pulp and seeds are edible

Mango and galia melons are deliciously sweet, and ripe ones should be firm, but yielding

Red chillies bring a dash of colour and spice to any dish

Lime accentuates flavours like a lemon, but it is a little more sour

Maple syrup, made from the sap of the maple tree, is smooth and rich

Fresh root ginger adds a delicious pungency to dishes with its distinct spiciness

Coriander has a distinct aromatic quality and is excellent in salsas

What could be lazier — or more welcome — on a hot summer's day than a soup that does not require any cooking? All that is needed is a little chopping and blending, followed by an hour or so of chilling. Be sure to use well-ripened fruit for this recipe.

INGREDIENTS

4 passion fruit, halved
1 ripe mango, diced
2.5cm (1 inch) piece fresh root ginger, grated
2 tbsp maple syrup (or corn syrup)
300ml (½ pint) fresh orange juice
½ tsp cracked black pepper

FOR THE SALSA

½ mango, cut in 5mm (¼ inch) dice
1 small wedge of ogen or galia melon, cut in 5mm (¼ inch) dice
¼ avocado, cut in 5mm (¼ inch) dice
1 tomato, skinned, deseeded, and chopped (see page 39)
1 small red onion, finely chopped
2 red chillies, deseeded and thinly sliced
2 tbsp chopped fresh coriander
pinch cayenne pepper
zest and juice of 2 limes

1 Scoop the seeds from the passion fruit into a bowl. Add the mango and ginger, cover, and leave to marinate for 1 hour at room temperature.

2 Meanwhile, for the salsa, blend together all the ingredients in a bowl; set aside.

3 Place the passion fruit, mango, and ginger in a blender or food processor, and add the maple syrup and orange juice. Blend to a fine purée, then strain through a fine strainer or sieve into a bowl. Cover and chill for 2 hours in the refrigerator.

4 To serve, add the salsa to the blended soup, sprinkle with a little cracked black pepper, and serve in individual, well-chilled bowls.

🕐 **Preparation time**
20 minutes, plus 1 hour marinating time, plus 2 hours chilling time

Serves 4

♡ **Nutritional notes**
kcalories 144; protein 2g; carbohydrate 30g; total fat 2g, of which saturated fat 0.5g; fibre 3g; sodium 29mg

EARLY SUMMER BASIL SOUP

The better the quality of the basil the better this simple, yet sophisticated, soup will be. Try to buy one of the large bunches of basil with a heady scent and pungent, peppery leaves that are sold loose in markets or Italian delicatessens.

INGREDIENTS

50g (1¾oz) butter

400g (14oz) young leeks, roughly chopped

2 celery sticks, roughly chopped

1.2 litres (2 pints) Vegetable Stock (see page 44)

zest and juice of ½ lemon

leaves from 1 large bunch fresh basil, plus extra, to garnish

6 tbsp double cream, plus extra, to serve

salt and freshly ground pepper

1 Heat the butter in a large pan, add the leeks and celery, cover, and sweat for 5–10 minutes over a medium heat. Remove the lid. Add the stock and lemon zest and juice. Bring to the boil, reduce the heat, and simmer for 15 minutes.

2 Remove from the heat, add the basil, and blend in a blender or food processor until smooth. Chill for 1 hour. Stir in the cream and adjust the seasoning. Serve chilled, with a generous swirl of cream, and garnished with basil leaves.

Preparation & cooking time
40 minutes, plus 1 hour for the stock, plus 1 hour chilling time

Serves 4

Nutritional notes
kcalories 354; protein 3g; carbohydrate 5g; total fat 36g, of which saturated fat 23g; fibre 2g; sodium 223mg

CHICKPEA & CHARD MINESTRONE WITH PESTO

If you cannot find red chard (sometimes known as ruby or rhubarb chard) Swiss chard is fine to use instead. Make this soup in full summer, when basil is plentiful and well flavoured.

INGREDIENTS

2 tbsp olive oil

1 onion, chopped

2 celery sticks, chopped

2 garlic cloves, crushed

½ tsp dried oregano

1 carrot, diced

50g (1¾oz) red chard, chopped

1 litre (1¾ pints) Dark Vegetable Stock, (see page 44)

200g (7oz) can chopped tomatoes

¼ tsp dried chilli flakes

50g (1¾oz) spaghetti

1 courgette, diced

50g (1¾oz) French beans, thinly sliced

1 potato, diced

50g (1¾oz) frozen peas

125g (4½oz) can chickpeas, drained

FOR THE PESTO

75g (2¾oz) basil leaves

2 garlic cloves

1 tbsp pine kernels

2 tbsp freshly grated Parmesan

pinch granulated sugar

75ml (2½fl oz) extra virgin olive oil

salt and freshly ground pepper

1 For the pesto, place all the ingredients except the olive oil in a blender or food processor and blend until smooth. With the motor still running, slowly add the oil until the pesto is smooth and has a grainy, slightly runny texture. Season to taste.

2 For the minestrone, heat the oil in a heavy-bottomed pan. Add the onion, celery, garlic, and oregano. Sauté over a medium heat for 2–3 minutes until soft. Add the carrot and chard, and cook for 1 minute until the chard has wilted.

3 Stir in the stock, tomatoes, and chilli flakes, and bring to the boil. Reduce the heat and simmer for 50–60 minutes. Break the spaghetti into 2.5cm (1 inch) lengths and add to the soup with the courgette, French beans, potato, peas, and chickpeas. Simmer over a medium heat for 15 minutes, stirring occasionally, until the vegetables are tender.

4 Pour the soup into four individual serving bowls. Place a tablespoon of the pesto in each bowl and serve hot.

Preparation & cooking time
1¾ hours, plus 1 hour for the stock

Serves 4

Nutritional notes
kcalories 432; protein 11g; carbohydrate 31g; total fat 30g, of which saturated fat 5g; fibre 5g; sodium 285mg

PARSNIP & WILD RICE MULLIGATAWNY

Parsnips, curry spices, and apples are one of those unexpectedly delicious combinations that just work perfectly together. The wild rice gives a wonderful texture and body to this complex and sustaining soup.

INGREDIENTS

50g (1¾oz) wild rice
50g (1¾oz) butter
1 onion, chopped
1 garlic clove, crushed
450g (1lb) parsnips, diced
½ tsp turmeric
2 tbsp curry powder
1.5 litres (2¼ pints) Vegetable Stock (see page 44)
1 green apple, peeled and diced
125ml (4fl oz) unsweetened coconut milk
4 tbsp chopped fresh coriander leaves
salt and freshly ground pepper

1 Place the wild rice in a large pan. Add 450ml (16fl oz) of water, or enough to cover the rice, bring to the boil, reduce the heat, and simmer for 30–40 minutes until the rice is tender. Drain.

2 Heat the butter in a separate pan. Add the onion and garlic and fry over a low heat for 5 minutes until soft. Add the parsnips, turmeric, and curry powder, and cook for a further 2–3 minutes, to allow the spices to release their fragrances.

3 Pour in the stock and add the diced apple. Stir well, then simmer for 40 minutes until the parsnips are tender.

4 Purée the ingredients until smooth in a blender or food processor. Strain through a coarse strainer or sieve, and season to taste. Return the soup to the pan and stir in the coconut milk, reserving 4 tablespoons. Bring almost to boiling point, remove from the heat, and stir in the wild rice and coriander. Serve with a swirl of reserved coconut milk.

🕐 **Preparation & cooking time**
1¼ hours, plus 1 hour for the stock

◎ **Serves 4**

♡ **Nutritional notes**
kcalories 251; protein 4g; carbohydrate 33g; total fat 12g, of which saturated fat 7g; fibre 7g; sodium 257mg

POTATO, SPINACH & SAFFRON SOUP

Here, fresh spinach and potatoes are cooked in a saffron-infused broth. Quail's eggs are then poached directly in the broth for an elegant presentation.

INGREDIENTS

1.5 litres (2¼ pints) Vegetable Stock (see page 44) or water
2 pinches saffron
250g (9oz) spinach leaves
2 tbsp olive oil
½ onion, chopped
1 garlic clove, crushed
250g (9oz) small new potatoes, peeled and sliced
4 quail's eggs
salt and freshly cracked pepper
freshly grated nutmeg

1 Pour the stock into a large pan, sprinkle in the saffron, and bring to the boil. Reduce the heat and simmer for 10 minutes to infuse the stock with the saffron. Remove from the heat.

2 Blanch the spinach leaves in a pan of boiling, salted water for 2 minutes, then immediately refresh in iced water. Drain and squeeze out any excess moisture.

3 Heat the oil in a pan, add the onion and garlic, and sweat over a medium heat for 2–3 minutes until soft. Stir in the spinach and cook for 2 minutes. Pour in the stock and bring to the boil. Add the potatoes, reduce the heat, and simmer for 15–20 minutes until the potatoes are tender. Season with salt, pepper, and nutmeg.

4 Crack the eggs into the soup, making sure that there is space between each one. Poach the eggs for 1 minute until set. Ladle the soup into individual bowls, adding a poached egg to each bowl.

🕐 **Preparation & cooking time**
1 hour, plus 1 hour for the stock

◎ **Serves 4**

♡ **Nutritional notes**
kcalories 145; protein 6g; carbohydrate 13g; total fat 9g, of which saturated fat 2g; fibre 2g; sodium 222mg

Grilled Vegetable Gazpacho

GRILLED VEGETABLE GAZPACHO

Serve this soup as it is for a rustic, smoky flavour, or stir in a spoonful of mayonnaise or double cream just before serving. Ketchup adds an extra sweetness, but you can substitute a tablespoon of tomato purée if you prefer.

INGREDIENTS

400g (14oz) ripe, but firm, plum tomatoes

1 red pepper, halved and deseeded

1 green pepper, halved and deseeded

1 red onion, cut in 5mm (¼ inch) rings

6 tbsp olive oil

2 slices white bread, soaked in water for 10 minutes, then squeezed out

½ cucumber, chopped

2 garlic cloves, sliced

2 tbsp red wine vinegar

1 tbsp fresh oregano leaves

4 fresh basil leaves, plus extra, to garnish

¼ tsp ground cumin

½ tsp granulated sugar

3 tbsp tomato ketchup

salt and freshly ground pepper

croutons, to serve

1 Brush the tomatoes, peppers, and onion with 2 tablespoons of the olive oil. Preheat the grill to hot and grill the vegetables for 10 minutes, turning occasionally, until lightly charred all over; cool.

2 When cold, dice the vegetables finely. Place in a large bowl, reserving 2 tablespoons. Crumble the bread into the bowl, then add the cucumber, garlic, vinegar, 300ml (½ pint) water, herbs, cumin, and the remaining oil. Season, add the sugar and ketchup, and leave to marinate for at least 6 hours in the refrigerator.

3 Blend to a fine purée in a blender or food processor. Strain through a coarse strainer. Serve well chilled, in individual bowls, with the reserved vegetables and a few croutons sprinkled on top. Garnish with basil leaves.

Preparation & cooking time
40 minutes, plus at least 6 hours marinating time (preferably overnight)

Serves 4

Nutritional notes
kcalories 127; protein 5g; carbohydrate 26g; total fat 1g, of which saturated fat 0.3g; fibre 4g; sodium 390mg

BUTTERNUT SOUP WITH CINNAMON CREAM

With its sweet, nutty flavour and smooth texture, butternut squash can be used to make one of the best winter soups. Serve the soup hot, and top each serving with a dollop of orange- and cinnamon-scented cream for a sophisticated finish.

INGREDIENTS

2 tbsp olive oil

1 onion, finely chopped

750g (1lb 10oz) butternut squash, chopped

1 carrot, chopped

4cm (1½ inch) piece fresh root ginger, grated

½ tsp ground cinnamon

1 tbsp ground coriander

700ml (1¼ pints) Vegetable Stock (see page 44)

300ml (½ pint) milk

2 tbsp semolina

salt and freshly ground pepper

FOR THE CINNAMON CREAM

100ml (3½fl oz) double cream

1 tsp grated orange zest

1 tsp ground cinnamon

1 In a heavy-bottomed pan, heat the olive oil and fry the onion over a medium heat for 5 minutes until golden. Add the squash, carrot, ginger, cinnamon, and coriander. Sauté over a medium heat, stirring, for 5–8 minutes until the vegetables are browned.

2 Add the stock and milk, and bring to the boil. Reduce the heat to medium, stir in the semolina, and cook, stirring, for 30–35 minutes until the vegetables are tender. Blend until smooth in a blender or food processor. Season.

3 For the cinnamon cream, lightly whisk together the cream, orange zest, and cinnamon until the mixture forms soft peaks. Serve the soup hot, topped with a spoonful of cinnamon cream.

Preparation & cooking time
1¼ hours, plus 1 hour for the stock

Serves 4

Nutritional notes
kcalories 327; protein 7g; carbohydrate 31g; total fat 21g, of which saturated fat 10g; fibre 4g; sodium 165mg

ROASTED CARROT SOUP WITH THAI FLAVOURS

Thai flavourings, such as lemongrass, ginger, and coriander, can transform the humble carrot into an exotic treat. Try this recipe using parsnips instead of carrots — it will work equally well.

INGREDIENTS

6 tbsp vegetable oil
450g (1lb) carrots, diced
25g (1oz) butter
1 onion, chopped
2 garlic cloves, chopped
2.5cm (1 inch) piece fresh root ginger, chopped
1 stick lemongrass, finely chopped
1 red chilli, finely sliced
½ tsp curry powder
1 tsp coriander seeds
400ml (14fl oz) can coconut milk
700ml (1½ pints) Vegetable Stock (see page 44)
2 tbsp lime juice
2 tbsp chopped fresh coriander
salt and freshly ground pepper

1 Heat the oil in an ovenproof dish and roast the carrots for 20–25 minutes until lightly golden and tender. Set aside.

2 Melt the butter in a large pan, add the onion, garlic, ginger, lemongrass, chilli, curry powder, and coriander, and cook over a low heat for 5 minutes to allow the spices to release their fragrances.

3 Stir in the roasted carrots, coconut milk, and stock, and bring to the boil. Reduce the heat to low and simmer gently for 8–10 minutes. Remove from the heat and season to taste. Add the lime juice and coriander and stir well. Serve hot.

Oven preheated to 200°C/400°F/Gas 6

Preparation & cooking time
50 minutes, plus 1 hour for the stock

Serves 4

Nutritional notes
kcalories 275; protein 2g; carbohydrate 18g; total fat 22g, of which saturated fat 5g; fibre 3g; sodium 287mg

BLACK BEAN SOUP WITH CHILLI SOFRITO

This thick, inky soup is served with a vivid splash of chunky green relish. As well as being perfect for soups, black beans make delicious additions to salads, or they can be mashed and served in tortillas with a spicy salsa.

INGREDIENTS

50g (1¾oz) butter
1 onion, chopped
2 celery sticks, chopped
1 small leek, chopped
2 garlic cloves, crushed
1 bay leaf
½ tsp ground cumin
¼ tsp aniseed seeds
1 tbsp chopped fresh oregano
375g (13oz) dried black beans, soaked overnight (see page 41)
juice of 1 lemon
salt and freshly ground pepper
4 tbsp crème fraîche, to serve

FOR THE SOFRITO

2 tbsp olive oil
2 spring onions, chopped
1 garlic clove, crushed
½ green pepper, cored, deseeded, and chopped
150g (5½oz) fresh coriander, chopped
1 small green chilli, halved and deseeded

1 Heat the butter in a medium pan. Add the onion, celery, leek, and garlic, and fry over a medium heat for 5 minutes. Add the bay leaf, cumin, aniseed, and oregano, and reduce the heat to low. Cook the vegetables for 10–12 minutes until tender.

2 Add the beans and 1.5 litres (2¾ pints) water, and bring to the boil. Lower the heat, then simmer for 1¼–1½ hours until the beans are tender.

3 Remove from the heat and purée in small batches in a blender or food processor until smooth. Add salt, pepper, and lemon juice to taste.

4 For the sofrito, blend all the ingredients to a coarse pulp in a blender or food processor. Season to taste. Serve the soup in hot bowls. Top each serving with a spoonful of crème fraîche and a generous spoonful of sofrito.

Preparation & cooking time
2¼ hours, plus overnight soaking time

Serves 4

Nutritional notes
kcalories 474; protein 27g; carbohydrate 46g; total fat 20g, of which saturated fat 10g; fibre 2g; sodium 260mg

CHILLED CUCUMBER & BULGAR WHEAT SOUP

The well-known Lebanese bulgar wheat salad, tabbouleh, provided the inspiration for this refreshing chilled soup. Half the cucumber is lightly cooked to enhance its delicate flavour without destroying its freshness. The remaining cucumber is served raw in the tabbouleh topping.

INGREDIENTS

2 cucumbers, peeled, deseeded, and chopped

25g (1oz) butter

1 medium leek, sliced

1 garlic clove, crushed

1 tsp chopped fresh oregano or ½ tsp dried

450ml (16fl oz) Vegetable Stock (see page 44)

150ml (¼ pint) double cream

150ml (¼ pint) natural yogurt

1 tsp Dijon mustard

juice of ½ lemon

salt and freshly ground pepper

FOR THE TABBOULEH

100g (3½oz) bulgar wheat

1 onion, chopped

2 tbsp chopped fresh flatleaf parsley

2 tbsp chopped fresh mint

8 pitted black olives, finely chopped

4 tbsp lemon juice

4 tbsp olive oil

1 tomato, skinned, deseeded (see page 39), and diced

1 For the tabbouleh, soak the bulgar wheat in a bowl of cold water for 1 hour. Drain, then squeeze out any excess water. Spread out on a clean cloth to dry.

2 Put the cucumber in a bowl and sprinkle with salt. After 30 minutes, rinse and pat dry.

3 Heat the butter in a pan. Add the leek, half the cucumber, and the garlic. Sweat over a medium heat for about 5 minutes. Add the oregano, stock, cream, and yogurt, and blend in a blender or food processor. Add the remaining soup ingredients and blend until smooth. Strain and chill.

4 For the tabbouleh, mix the onion, parsley, mint, olives, and remaining cucumber in a bowl with the bulgar wheat. Mix in the remaining ingredients, then season. Pile a tablespoon of tabbouleh in each bowl and ladle in the soup.

Preparation & cooking time
1 hour 40 minutes, plus 1 hour for the stock

Serves 4

Nutritional notes
kcalories 469; protein 7g; carbohydrate 28g; total fat 37g, of which saturated fat 17g; fibre 2g; sodium 393mg

LEBANESE GREEN LENTIL SOUP WITH MINT OIL

This soup is a godsend to anyone who finds that their home-grown mint annually runs riot and threatens to take over their whole garden. The mint oil is not only a nice addition to this soup, but it also makes a good dressing for pasta or salad.

INGREDIENTS

2 tbsp olive oil

1 onion, chopped

2 garlic cloves, crushed

250g (9oz) Puy lentils, soaked for 3 hours

2 tbsp cumin seeds

½ tsp coriander seeds

200g (7oz) can chopped tomatoes

½ tbsp tomato purée

1.5 litres (2¼ pints) Vegetable Stock (see page 44)

juice of ½ lemon

salt and freshly ground pepper

pinch of cayenne pepper

FOR THE MINT OIL

handful of fresh mint leaves

4 tbsp olive oil

1 Heat the oil in a pan, add the onion and garlic, and sweat over a medium heat for 10 minutes until soft. Add the lentils, cumin, and coriander seeds, and fry over a medium heat for 5–10 minutes. Add the tomatoes, tomato purée, and stock. Bring to the boil, then reduce the heat and simmer for 40 minutes until the lentils are soft.

2 Blend to a smooth purée in a blender or food processor. Stir in the lemon juice and season with salt, pepper, and cayenne pepper.

3 For the mint oil, place the mint and olive oil in a blender or food processor and blend to a coarse purée. Serve the soup hot with a swirl of the mint oil on top.

Preparation & cooking time
1 hour 10 minutes, plus 3 hours soaking time, plus 1 hour for the stock

Serves 4

Nutritional notes
kcalories 361; protein 17g; carbohydrate 36g; total fat 19g, of which saturated fat 3g; fibre 7g; sodium 138mg

SMOKY CORN VELOUTE

You will need fresh corn on the cob for this recipe. You can grill it under the grill or on a barbecue for that uniquely smoky taste. To enhance the flavour of the stock, even the cores are used in this recipe.

INGREDIENTS

4 corn on the cob

1.5 litres (2¾ pints) Vegetable Stock (see page 44)

2 tbsp olive oil

40g (1½oz) butter

1 onion, chopped

1 garlic clove, crushed

1 leek, chopped

4 corn tortillas, chopped

salt and freshly ground pepper

TO FINISH THE SOUP

100ml (3½fl oz) double cream, plus extra, to serve

1 egg yolk

75g (2¾oz) Cheddar, coarsely grated

2 corn tortillas, cut in strips and deep-fried

1 Grill the corn cobs under a hot grill for 15 minutes, turning them until charred, but not burnt.

2 Scrape off the kernels with a knife and reserve. Chop the cores and place in a pan. Cover with the stock, bring to the boil, reduce the heat, and simmer for 45 minutes. Strain off the stock and set aside; discard the cores.

3 Heat the oil and butter in a pan. Add the onion, garlic, leek, and tortillas, and fry over a medium heat for 3–4 minutes. Reduce the heat and add the corn kernels. Pour in the stock, and simmer for 45 minutes, stirring often. Blend until smooth in a blender or food processor. Season.

4 To finish the soup, gently whisk together the cream and egg yolk. Add one ladleful of soup, whisk, then return to the pan. Heat through, then transfer to four bowls. Top each bowl with Cheddar, fried tortilla strips, and a swirl of cream.

Preparation & cooking time
2¼ hours, plus 1 hour for the stock

Serves 4

Nutritional notes
kcalories 694; protein 18g; carbohydrate 77g; total fat 37g, of which saturated fat 19g; fibre 6g; sodium 545mg

Note: this recipe contains lightly cooked egg.

HOT & SOUR VEGETABLE SOUP

In China, soup is a very important part of any meal, and this particular soup is one of the most popular in China. You may need to go to an Oriental food store to buy the dried Chinese mushrooms, but all the other ingredients are available from supermarkets. The white wine vinegar adds the sour note to the soup.

INGREDIENTS

2 tbsp sesame oil

8 spring onions, sliced

150g (5½oz) carrots, finely shredded

2.5cm (1 inch) piece fresh root ginger, finely shredded

1 garlic clove, crushed

700ml (1¼ pints) Dark Vegetable Stock (see page 44)

4 dried Chinese black mushrooms

1 pak choi, shredded

4 tbsp ketjap manis (Indonesian soy sauce)

2 tbsp white wine vinegar

1 tsp caster sugar

1 tsp chilli oil

1 tbsp cornflour, mixed to a paste with 2 tbsp cold water

1 egg, lightly beaten

50g (1¼oz) firm tofu, cut in 5mm (¼ inch) cubes

1 Heat the sesame oil in a large pan over a high heat until hot, then add half the spring onions, the carrots, ginger, and garlic. Reduce the heat to medium and cook, stirring, for 5 minutes. Add the stock and bring to the boil. Add the dried Chinese black mushrooms and simmer for 10 minutes, then add the pak choi.

2 In a bowl, combine the ketjap manis with the vinegar, sugar, chilli oil, and cornflour paste. Mix together to form a paste.

3 Add the mixture to the soup, stir in, and bring to the boil. Boil for 1 minute. Gradually add the beaten egg to the soup, stirring gently so that it forms thin strands. Add the tofu, scatter the remaining spring onion on top, and serve hot.

Preparation & cooking time
40 minutes, plus 1 hour for the stock

Serves 4

Nutritional notes
kcalories 178; protein 6g; carbohydrate 19g; total fat 9g. of which saturated fat 1g; fibre 2g; sodium 901mg

ROASTED RED PEPPER & ZHUG SOUP

Zhug is a fiery hot relish from Yemen, made with coriander, garlic, and masses of chilli. It is usually served as an accompaniment to grilled food, but here it forms the base of this vivid soup.

INGREDIENTS

4 red peppers, roasted, peeled, and deseeded (see page 39)

600ml (1 pint) Vegetable Stock (see page 44)

150ml (¼ pint) tomato passata

4 tbsp fresh coriander leaves

1 tbsp balsamic vinegar

1 tbsp honey

salt and freshly ground pepper

FOR THE ZHUG

3 garlic cloves, roughly chopped

½ tsp coriander seeds

½ tsp cumin seeds

2 red chillies, halved and deseeded

4 tbsp olive oil

1 large onion, grated

1 For the zhug, dry roast the garlic, coriander, cumin, and chillies in a dry frying pan, over a low heat, for 5 minutes. Add the oil, stir in the onion, and continue to cook for a further 10 minutes. Set aside to cool.

2 Place the zhug in a blender or food processor. Add the roasted peppers, 6 tablespoons of the vegetable stock, the passata, and the fresh coriander, and blend to a purée.

3 Place the soup in a large pan and heat through over a medium heat, stirring occasionally. Stir in the remaining vegetable stock and season to taste with salt and pepper. Finally, add the vinegar and honey. Stir the soup well and serve hot.

Preparation & cooking time
1 hour, plus 1 hour for the stock

Serves 4

Nutritional notes
kcalories 200; protein 3g; carbohydrate 21g; total fat 12g, of which saturated fat 2g; fibre 4g; sodium 109mg

TARTS & PIES

ORIGINALLY CONCEIVED for convenience, the wrapping of food in pastry or dough has been elevated to an art form. These recipes demonstrate the versatility of pastry, from crispy filo to delicate brioche dough and buttery shortcrust. They show how pastry can be combined with the exciting flavours and textures of fresh green leaves, succulent roast vegetables, herbs, cheeses, and warming spices. You can serve any of these dishes as a centrepiece for a special meal, or for an informal family supper.

SPINACH, BASIL & PUMPKIN RICE TORTE

KEY INGREDIENTS

Filo pastry is available in thin sheets and has a light, delicate texture

Spinach is flavoursome and colourful; it is ideal with cream or cheese

Parmesan with risotto is a classic combination

Arborio, the risotto rice, comes from Piedmont, Northern Italy

Pumpkin lends sweetness and colour to many dishes

Fresh basil gives the true taste of Italian cookery

This recipe is a variation on a classic Italian staple, Torta de Riso, or Rice Tart, which originated in Piedmont. I truly love the simplicity and rustic character of this dish. Throughout Italy there are many variations; my favourite includes layers of sliced, hard-boiled eggs and slices of mozzarella between the layers of rice. Serve warm with Roasted Cherry Tomato Salsa (see page 45).

INGREDIENTS

| 2 tbsp olive oil |
| 1 onion, thinly sliced |
| 400g (14oz) fresh spinach |
| handful fresh basil leaves, chopped |
| 200g (7oz) Arborio rice, cooked |
| 100g (3½oz) Parmesan, grated |
| 2 eggs, lightly beaten |
| 50g (1¾oz) butter, melted |
| 9 sheets filo pastry, halved |
| 625g (1lb 6oz) pumpkin, peeled, cut into 8mm (⅜ inch) slices, and boiled |
| salt and freshly ground pepper |

1 Heat the oil in a frying pan and fry the onion over a medium to low heat for 5 minutes until golden. Add the spinach and basil and cook for 2 minutes until wilted. Chop finely, then place in a tea towel and squeeze out excess moisture. Divide the rice equally between two bowls, add the spinach to one, and divide the Parmesan and eggs between the two bowls. Mix well.

2 Grease a 20cm (8 inch) springform cake tin with a little butter. Brush the sheets of filo pastry with butter and use to line the base and sides of the cake tin, leaving a small overhang of filo. Reserve six half-sheets of filo for the top (keep them under a damp cloth until ready to use).

3 Layer the torte: place the spinach rice in the base, followed by the pumpkin, with the remaining rice on top; season each layer. Cut the reserved pastry into strips, brush with butter, and use to decorate the torte. Bake for 50 minutes until golden. Turn out of the tin on to a baking sheet and bake for a few minutes longer to crisp the sides. Cool a little before serving.

Oven preheated to 190°C/375°F/Gas 5

Preparation & cooking time 1½–1¾ hours

Serves 8

Nutritional notes kcalories 210; protein 10g; carbohydrate 11g; total fat 14g, of which saturated fat 7g; fibre 2g; sodium 384mg

SALSIFY & WILD MUSHROOM TART

Salsify is a much-neglected vegetable and deserves wider recognition. Its delicate flavour is complemented by the walnut pastry in this tart. If you cannot find salsify, however, asparagus, blanched leeks, or celeriac also work very well.

INGREDIENTS

FOR THE WALNUT PASTRY

250g (9oz) plain flour, plus extra, to dust

pinch of salt

60g (2¼ oz) ground walnuts

135g (4¾ oz) unsalted butter, chilled and cut in cubes, plus extra, to grease

1 egg, beaten

FOR THE FILLING

juice of ½ lemon

150g (5½oz) salsify, peeled and cut diagonally in 2cm (¾ inch) lengths

25g (1oz) butter

100g (3½oz) oyster mushrooms, chopped

50g (1¾oz) sliced porcini mushrooms, soaked overnight in 125ml (4fl oz) water

120ml (3¾fl oz) double cream

1 egg, beaten

1 tbsp chopped fresh flatleaf parsley

salt and freshly ground pepper

selection of lamb's lettuce and frisée, to serve

FOR THE MUSTARD VINAIGRETTE

3 tbsp olive oil

1 tbsp walnut oil

1 tbsp champagne or white wine vinegar

1 tsp wholegrain mustard

1 tbsp redcurrant jelly

1 For the pastry, sift the flour and salt into a bowl and mix in the walnuts. Rub in the butter until the mixture resembles fine breadcrumbs. Stir in the egg to bind. Gather the pastry together and roll into a ball, cover, and leave to chill for 1 hour.

2 For the filling, bring a large pan of water to the boil, add the lemon juice, and poach the salsify for 4–5 minutes. Drain.

3 Heat the butter in a frying pan and fry the oyster mushrooms over a medium heat for 2–3 minutes until tender. Drain the porcini, reserving the soaking liquid, and add the porcini to the pan. Season lightly and set aside. Mix together the cream, egg, parsley, and reserved porcini soaking liquid. Season to taste and set aside.

4 Roll out the pastry on a lightly floured work surface and use to line four lightly greased, individual 7cm (2¾ inch) tart tins. Prick the bases with a fork, cover with greaseproof paper, and fill with baking beans. Bake blind for 5–6 minutes. Remove the beans and paper, and leave to cool.

5 Arrange the salsify and mushrooms in the bases of the tart shells, then pour in the cream mixture to fill each shell. Bake for 12–15 minutes until the pastry is golden and the filling has just set.

6 For the vinaigrette, blend all the ingredients together well. Arrange a bed of lamb's lettuce and frisée on each of four serving plates and drizzle with the vinaigrette. Place one tart on top of each bed of salad and serve while still warm.

Oven preheated to
200°C/400°F/Gas 6

Preparation & cooking time
2 hours, plus overnight soaking time

Serves 4

Nutritional notes
kcalories 953; protein 15g; carbohydrate 63g; total fat 73g, of which saturated fat 34g; fibre 4g; sodium 597mg

HIGH-RISE PASTA PIE

This impressive pasta pie first caught my eye in Italy, where it was filled with pasta bound in a thick ragu sauce (tomato and meat-based sauce). I experimented with the recipe and have come up with my own vegetarian version. It is great for an informal buffet-style lunch or a dinner party and tastes equally good served hot or cold.

INGREDIENTS

675g (1lb 8oz) Shortcrust Pastry (see page 42)

225g (8oz) macaroni or penne pasta

50g (1¼ oz) butter, plus extra, to grease

350g (12oz) chard leaves, roughly shredded

125g (4½oz) chestnut mushrooms, quartered

50g (1¾ oz) sun-dried tomatoes, roughly chopped

25g (1oz) pine kernels, toasted

50g (1¾ oz) frozen peas, defrosted

1 tbsp cornflour or arrowroot, mixed to a paste with 2 tbsp cold water

300ml (½ pint) double cream

3 eggs, beaten

salt and freshly ground pepper

freshly grated nutmeg

1 Lightly grease a 22cm (8½ inch) springform cake tin. On a lightly floured work surface, roll out two-thirds of the pastry and use to line the cake tin.

2 Cook the pasta in plenty of boiling, salted water according to packet instructions until al dente. Drain and season with salt, pepper, and nutmeg.

3 Melt the butter in a large pan, add the chard, and sweat over a medium heat for 4–5 minutes until tender. Add the mushrooms and tomatoes, and cook for 1 minute. Remove from the heat and toss together with the pasta. Add the pine kernels and peas, mix well, and adjust the seasoning.

4 Place the pasta in the pastry case and press down lightly. Combine the cornflour paste with the cream and eggs in a bowl, then pour the cream mixture over the pasta in the tin.

5 Roll out the remaining pastry into a circle large enough to cover the pie. Dampen the edges of the pastry with water, then top the pie with the pastry circle. Crimp and seal the edges by pressing with your thumb and forefinger all the way around. Score a criss-cross pattern on the top.

6 Make a small hole in the top for steam to escape. Bake for 1¼–1½ hours until the pastry is golden and the middle is set. Leave to rest for 10–15 minutes before serving. Serve hot or cold.

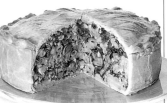

Oven preheated to 190°C/375°F/Gas 5

Preparation & cooking time 2¼–2½ hours, plus 40 minutes for the pastry

Serves 8

Nutritional notes kcalories 836; protein 14g; carbohydrate 59g; total fat 62g, of which saturated fat 35g; fibre 3g; sodium 321mg

TUSCAN ROLL

Filled with roasted vegetables, mozzarella, sun-dried tomatoes, and olive paste, this colourful loaf is imbued with the irresistible flavours and aromas of Italy. Use a good olive oil for roasting the vegetables to give them a superb taste. You can make the Tuscan Roll ahead and freeze it, uncooked, for up to three months. Olivada is an olive spread, great for adding extra flavour to dishes.

Oven preheated to
200°C/400°F/Gas 6

Preparation & cooking time
2 hours

Serves 8

Nutritional notes
kcalories 384; protein 11g;
carbohydrate 30g;
total fat 25g, of which
saturated fat 5g;
fibre 4g; sodium 629mg

INGREDIENTS

FOR THE DOUGH

250g (9oz) strong plain white flour,
plus extra, to dust

7g (¹⁄₂ oz) sachet easy-blend yeast

¹⁄₂ tsp salt

150ml (¹⁄₄ pint) tepid water

1 tbsp olive oil, plus extra, to grease

FOR THE FILLING

1 aubergine, cut in 1cm (¹⁄₂ inch) slices

1 onion, sliced

4 courgettes (2 yellow, 2 green) cut
in 1cm (¹⁄₂ inch) slices

2 medium fennel, cut in wedges

6 tbsp olive oil

150g (5¹⁄₂oz) sun-dried tomatoes

4 tbsp Olivada (see page 45)

2 garlic cloves, crushed

300g (10¹⁄₂oz) Swiss chard or spinach

125g (4¹⁄₂oz) cow's milk mozzarella,
thinly sliced

salt and freshly ground pepper

1 For the dough, stir together the flour, yeast, and salt in a large mixing bowl. Make a well in the centre and pour in the water and oil. Mix until all the liquid has been absorbed. Knead the dough on a lightly floured work surface for 2–3 minutes until smooth and elastic.

2 Place the dough in an oiled bowl, cover with a cloth and leave in a warm place until doubled in size, about 20–25 minutes.

3 For the filling, place the aubergine, onion, courgettes, and fennel in a roasting tin, in separate rows. Drizzle with 4 tablespoons of oil, season with salt and pepper, and bake for 25–30 minutes until tender. Place half the sun-dried tomatoes in a blender or food processor and blend to a coarse purée. Mix with the olivada.

4 Heat the remaining oil in a pan and fry the garlic and Swiss chard for 3–4 minutes until wilted. Leave to cool. Place in a clean tea towel and squeeze out any excess moisture.

5 On a lightly floured work surface, roll out the dough into a rectangle measuring 25cm x 20cm (10 inches x 8 inches). Spread the olivada mixture over the dough, leaving a 2.5cm (1 inch) border all around. Lay half the aubergine on top, followed by the chard, then the fennel, the remaining sun-dried tomatoes, mozzarella, courgettes, and finally, the remaining aubergine. Season each layer.

6 Fold the two short edges of the dough over the filling. With the long edge towards you, roll the dough up to enclose the filling. Place seam-side down on a greased baking sheet. Bake for 30–35 minutes until golden. Leave to cool completely before cutting into thick slices and serving.

CEP, WALNUT & JERUSALEM ARTICHOKE PARCELS

This is an elegant and tasty dish that can provide a solution to the annual challenge of what to serve for a vegetarian Christmas meal. You could try combinations of different vegetables, and perhaps replace the Cheddar with Gruyère or Parmesan, and the walnuts with hazelnuts or cashews. The variations on fillings are endless, so experiment.

INGREDIENTS

150g (5½oz) long-grain brown rice
25g (1oz) butter
2 shallots, finely chopped
1 garlic clove, crushed
1 large leek, shredded
175g (6oz) ceps or large, flat mushrooms, sliced
150g (5½oz) Jerusalem artichokes, peeled and grated
1 tbsp chopped fresh thyme
4 basil leaves, shredded
150g (5½oz) fresh white breadcrumbs
50g (1¾oz) walnuts, chopped
100g (3½ oz) Cheddar, grated
2 eggs, plus 1 to seal and glaze, beaten
450g (1lb) ready-made puff pastry, defrosted if frozen
flour, to dust
salt and freshly ground pepper
pinch of nutmeg
sprigs fresh basil, to garnish
Madeira Sauce (see page 44), to serve

1 Boil the rice for 30–35 minutes, or according to packet instructions, until tender. Drain, place in a bowl, and leave to cool.

2 In a separate pan, heat the butter, add the shallots and garlic, and sauté for 5 minutes over a low heat until softened. Add the leek and, over a high heat, stir in the ceps, artichokes, and herbs. Sauté for about 5 minutes until golden. Leave to cool.

3 In a clean bowl, combine the rice, sautéed vegetables, breadcrumbs, walnuts, Cheddar, and 2 eggs. Season to taste with salt, pepper, and nutmeg.

4 On a lightly floured work surface, roll out the pastry to a rectangle about 3mm (⅛ inch) thick. Trim to 30cm x 20cm (12 x 8 inches), then cut into six 10cm (4 inch) squares.

5 Form the rice mixture into balls, each about the size of a golf ball. Place one in the centre of each pastry square, and form the parcels (see steps 1–3 below).

6 Brush the outside of each parcel with beaten egg and leave in the refrigerator until ready to bake. Bake for 15–20 minutes until golden. Garnish with basil and serve with Madeira sauce.

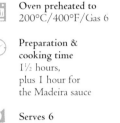

Oven preheated to
200°C/400°F/Gas 6

Preparation & cooking time
1½ hours, plus 1 hour for the Madeira sauce

Serves 6

Nutritional notes
kcalories 705; protein 18g; carbohydrate 54g; total fat 48g, of which saturated fat 11g; fibre 3g; sodium 528mg

MAKING THE PARCELS

1 *Place a rice ball, about the size of a golf ball, in the centre of each pastry square. Brush the edges of the square with beaten egg.*

2 *Bring the four corners up to the centre, then press the edges together with your index fingers and thumbs to seal in the filling.*

3 *Roll out the pastry trimmings and cut out six circles, each about 4cm (1½ inches) in diameter. Place on the parcels and press down lightly to seal.*

PEPPER & DOLCELATTE TARTS

Dolcelatte and sage is an excellent combination, very popular in Italian cookery. With their multicoloured topping of roasted pepper strips, these little tarts make an eye-catching starter or delicious light lunch.

INGREDIENTS

250g (9oz) Shortcrust Pastry (see page 42)

5 tbsp olive oil, plus extra, to grease

2 red onions, thinly sliced

1 large garlic clove, crushed

1 tbsp chopped fresh sage

3 tbsp milk

100g (3½oz) dolcelatte

3 peppers (1 red, 1 green, 1 yellow) roasted, peeled, deseeded (see page 39), and cut in julienne strips

25g (1oz) pitted black olives, sliced

salt and freshly cracked black pepper

1 Lightly grease four individual 7cm (2¾ inch) tart tins. Roll out the pastry on a lightly floured work surface and use to line the tart tins. Prick the bases, line with greaseproof paper, and fill with baking beans. Leave the pastry to rest in a cool place for 15 minutes before baking.

2 Bake the pastry cases blind for 5–6 minutes, remove the baking beans and paper, and return the cases to the oven for 3–4 minutes until crisp. Leave to cool, then remove from the tins.

3 Heat 3 tablespoons of olive oil in a frying pan and fry the onions, garlic, and sage over a low heat for about 15 minutes until softened. Remove from the heat. Cream together the milk and the dolcelatte to make a thick sauce. Beat the cheese mixture into the onions until the cheese melts.

4 Season the mixture and divide it between the pastry cases, then arrange the roasted pepper strips on top, following the curve of the tarts. Dot with the olives, drizzle over the remaining oil, and sprinkle with pepper. Place on a baking sheet and return to the oven to heat through for 5 minutes, then serve warm.

Oven preheated to 190°C/375°F/Gas 5

Preparation & cooking time 1½ hours, plus 40 minutes for the pastry

Serves 4

Nutritional notes kcalories 559; protein 10g; carbohydrate 41g; total fat 40g, of which saturated fat 21g; fibre 3g; sodium 402mg

GOAN POTATO, PEA & MINT PASTIES

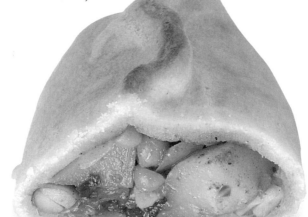

Chopped mint adds a refreshing note to the spicy filling in these little pasties. They are perfect for parties and can be prepared well ahead of time. You can freeze them uncooked for up to three months, then bake or fry them from frozen; just allow a few minutes longer for them to cook.

INGREDIENTS

FOR THE PASTRY DOUGH

250g (9oz) plain flour, plus extra, to dust

50g (1¾oz) chilled butter, cubed

75ml (2½fl oz) tepid milk

1 egg, beaten, to glaze

FOR THE FILLING

3 tbsp vegetable oil, plus extra for deep-frying, plus extra, to grease

1 onion, chopped

1 garlic clove, crushed

½ tsp turmeric

1 tsp ground cumin

1 tsp garam masala

good pinch ground ginger

½ tsp dried chilli flakes

250g (9oz) potatoes, diced

150g (5½oz) frozen peas

2 tbsp chopped fresh mint

salt and freshly ground pepper

fruit chutney or Tomato Raita (see page 147), to serve

Oven preheated to
200°C/400°F/Gas 6

Preparation & cooking time
1½–2 hours

Serves 8

Nutritional notes
kcalories 280; protein 8g;
carbohydrate 37g;
total fat 12g, of which
saturated fat 5g;
fibre 3g; sodium 145mg

1 For the pastry, sift the flour into a bowl, add the butter, and rub in until the mixture resembles fine breadcrumbs. Mix in the milk to form a soft dough. Turn out the dough on to a lightly floured surface and knead. Wrap in oiled clingfilm, and leave to chill in the refrigerator for 45 minutes.

2 For the filling, heat the oil in a frying pan, add the onion, garlic, and spices, and fry gently for 3–4 minutes. In a separate pan, deep-fry the potatoes for about 5 minutes until golden. Add the potatoes to the spices, and stir until well coated with the mixture.

3 Add boiling water to cover the mixture, reduce the heat, and simmer for 3–5 minutes. Add the peas and cook for a further 2–3 minutes. Remove from the heat, add the mint, season, and leave to cool.

4 Take the pastry out of the refrigerator and leave it to stand for 5 minutes before dividing it into eight pieces. On a lightly floured surface, roll each piece into a 13cm (5 inch) circle. Place a mound of filling in the centre of each circle, brush the border with beaten egg, then bring the pastry up over the filling. Press the edges together to seal. The parcels should resemble Cornish pasties.

5 Brush the pasties with the beaten egg, lay on a lightly greased baking sheet, and bake for 12–15 minutes. Alternatively, deep-fry the pasties in hot oil for 5 minutes. Serve with a fruit chutney or tomato raita.

PASTA & GNOCCHI

THE ACT OF TRANSFORMING just a few simple ingredients into golden sheets of pasta can be immensely satisfying. However, some recipes call for dried, ready-made pasta, such as penne. Always cook pasta and gnocchi in plenty of boiling, salted water, to which a little oil has been added to prevent them from sticking. Gnocchi are little dumplings. They are usually made with potatoes, but here, I have included some variations: gnocchi made with orange sweet potatoes, ricotta, and even olive bread.

— LAYERED STRACCHI WITH ROASTED VEGETABLES —

KEY INGREDIENTS

Red peppers are widely used for their colour and sweet taste

Courgettes need hardly any cooking; the smaller they are the more flavour they have

Fresh pasta has a different texture from dried pasta – you can buy it, but it is worth making your own

Aubergines are popular in Mediterranean countries and combine well with acidic foods

Garlic, plum tomatoes, basil, and pine nuts are delicious in pesto and other Mediterranean sauces

Stracchi, which means "rags" in Italian, describes perfectly these sheets of pasta, layered loosely with vegetables. The pasta is served with a pesto made with roasted tomatoes, which provide a mellow flavour.

INGREDIENTS

1 quantity basic pasta dough (see page 43)

1 onion, cut in 1cm (½ inch) rings

1 large aubergine, sliced

4 small tomatoes, halved

2 courgettes, sliced

4 tbsp olive oil

3 peppers (1 red, 1 yellow, 1 green), roasted, peeled, and deseeded (see page 39)

fresh chives, to garnish

FOR THE ROASTED TOMATO PESTO

4 garlic cloves, peeled

150ml (¼ pint) extra virgin olive oil

6 plum tomatoes, skinned (see page 39)

25g (1oz) fresh basil leaves

25g (1oz) pine nuts

2 tbsp freshly grated Parmesan

salt and freshly ground pepper

1 Roll out the pasta dough into thin sheets (see page 43), and cut into 12 rectangles, each 10cm x 7.5cm (4 inches x 3 inches).

2 Set the pasta sheets aside and preheat the grill. Brush all the vegetables except the peppers with some of the oil. Grill the oiled vegetables for 5 minutes on each side until charred and tender.

3 For the pesto, drizzle the garlic with 1 tablespoon of olive oil, and roast for 15 minutes. Roughly chop the tomatoes and add to the garlic. Roast for 15 minutes more.

4 Transfer the tomatoes and garlic to a blender or food processor. Purée with the remaining pesto ingredients. Season to taste and set aside.

5 Cook the pasta in boiling, salted water for 5 minutes until al dente; drain. Layer all the vegetables and the pesto between three sheets of pasta per person. Drizzle with oil and a little more pesto, then garnish with chives.

Oven preheated to 200°C/400°F/Gas 6

Preparation & cooking time 1 hour, plus 30 minutes for the pasta dough

Serves 4

Nutritional notes kcalories 904; protein 20g; carbohydrate 65g; total fat 65g, of which saturated fat 11g; fibre 8g; sodium 230mg

BUCKWHEAT LASAGNETTE WITH CABBAGE & CEPS

This is quite a complex dish, which involves making your own buckwheat pasta. However, I think you will find that the taste repays the effort. The lasagnette has a nutty, autumnal flavour, which complements the cabbage, mushrooms, and sage in the filling perfectly.

INGREDIENTS

FOR THE LASAGNETTE

200g (7oz) buckwheat flour

120g (4¼oz) strong plain flour, plus extra, to dust

2 eggs, plus 2 egg yolks, beaten together

2 tbsp olive oil

FOR THE FILLING

1 small savoy cabbage, shredded

50g (1¾oz) butter, plus extra, to grease

1 garlic clove, crushed

4 large fresh sage leaves

250g (9oz) ceps, sliced

salt and freshly ground pepper

freshly grated nutmeg

FOR THE SAUCE

200g (7oz) Pecorino sardo, grated

50g (1¾oz) butter

150ml (¼ pint) whipping cream

1 egg yolk

1 For the lasagnette, blend together the two flours on a clean surface. Make a well in the centre, pour in the eggs and oil, and gradually incorporate the flour to form a dough.

2 Work the dough until it feels moist but not sticky. Place in a bowl, cover with clingfilm, and leave to rest for 1 hour.

3 Roll out the pasta into thin sheets (see page 43). Cut into eight 20cm (8 inch) squares, then set aside on a floured tray to dry for about 10 minutes.

4 For the filling, blanch the cabbage for 3 minutes in boiling water; drain well. Heat the butter in a frying pan, then add the garlic and sage leaves. Add the ceps and the blanched cabbage, and cook over a medium heat for 4–5 minutes. Season with salt, pepper, and nutmeg.

5 Cook the pasta in boiling, salted water until al dente; drain. Season with salt, pepper, and nutmeg. Lay out the pasta on a flat work surface, spread with the cabbage and mushroom mixture, and roll each sheet up tightly. Cut each roll into small, equal-sized slices, and lay these flat in a lightly buttered, ovenproof dish. Set aside.

6 For the sauce, place the Pecorino, butter, and cream in a large, heatproof bowl over a pan of boiling water. Melt the Pecorino slowly, whisking occasionally. Season, add the egg yolk, and whisk until the sauce is smooth. Pour the sauce over the lasagnette. Bake for 15 minutes until golden.

Oven preheated to
200°C/400°F/Gas 6

Preparation & cooking time
1¼ hours, plus 1 hour resting time

Serves 4

Nutritional notes
kcalories 1000; protein 37g; carbohydrate 70g; total fat 66g, of which saturated fat 36g; fibre 5g; sodium 904mg

OLIVADA & MOZZARELLA STUFFED AUBERGINE

Stuffing aubergine slices with tagliatelle is easier than might be expected, as long as you use a two-pronged fork, such as a carving fork. Take a few pasta strands, roll them around the fork into a neat shape, then ease this off on to a slice of aubergine. If the pasta starts to stick before it is rolled, toss it in a little olive oil.

INGREDIENTS

175g (6oz) fresh tagliatelle (see page 43)

6 tbsp olive oil

1 garlic clove, crushed

2 aubergines, thinly sliced lengthways

4 tbsp Olivada (see page 45)

150g (5½oz) cow's milk mozzarella, grated

handful fresh basil leaves, shredded, plus extra, to garnish

150ml (¼ pint) Fresh Tomato Sauce (see page 45), optional

salt and freshly ground pepper

freshly grated nutmeg

1 Bring a large pan of salted water to the boil, and cook the tagliatelle for 3 minutes until al dente. Drain well, and return to the pan. Season with salt, pepper, and nutmeg, then leave to cool.

2 Heat the oil in a frying pan, then add the garlic and aubergine slices. Fry the aubergine over a medium heat for 5 minutes on each side until golden and tender. Drain any excess oil from the aubergine on kitchen paper.

3 Lay out the aubergine slices on a chopping board, spread each one with olivada, and top with grated mozzarella.

4 Roll a forkful of the cooked tagliatelle into a ball and place on top of the mozzarella. Sprinkle with the shredded basil leaves. Roll up each aubergine slice and secure with a cocktail stick.

5 Arrange the aubergine rolls in a single layer in a baking dish, and bake for 10–12 minutes. Transfer to a serving dish and add the tomato sauce, if using. Garnish with fresh basil.

Oven preheated to 180°C/350°F/Gas 4

Preparation & cooking time 1 hour, plus 40 minutes to make the tagliatelle

Serves 4

Nutritional notes kcalories 562; protein 18g; carbohydrate 32g; total fat 41g, of which saturated fat 10g; fibre 5g; sodium 638mg

PASTA WITH TOMATO, OLIVE & MELON SALSA

This is a wonderfully refreshing salad for a hot summer's day. Try it with the optional goat's cheese to make a substantial meal — goat's cheese goes remarkably well with melon.

INGREDIENTS

450g (1lb) spaghettini

2 Crottin Chavignol (goat's cheeses), cut in small dice (optional)

salt and freshly ground pepper

FOR THE SALSA

450g (1lb) ripe, but firm plum tomatoes, diced

½ cantaloupe melon, deseeded and diced

2 tbsp pitted black olives, diced

½ garlic clove, crushed

¼ tsp dried chilli flakes

150ml (¼ pint) extra virgin olive oil

1 For the salsa, place the diced tomatoes, melon, and olives in a bowl. Add the garlic, chilli flakes, and olive oil, season with salt and pepper, toss well to combine, and leave to marinate for 1 hour.

2 Cook the spaghettini in boiling, salted water according to packet instructions until al dente. Drain well, place in a large serving bowl, add the salsa, then toss well to combine. Scatter the diced goat's cheese on top, if using, and serve.

Preparation & cooking time 25 minutes, plus 1 hour marinating time

Serves 4

Nutritional notes kcalories 835; protein 19g; carbohydrate 92g; total fat 46g, of which saturated fat 10g; fibre 6g; sodium 587mg

SPINACH & CUMIN RAVIOLI WITH LEMON BUTTER

Cumin seeds add an unexpected, pleasant, spicy note to a classic filling of spinach and ricotta for these homemade ravioli.

INGREDIENTS

1 quantity basic pasta dough (see page 43)

FOR THE FILLING

25g (1oz) butter

1 garlic clove, crushed

1 tsp cumin seeds

250g (9oz) spinach, chopped

100g (3½oz) ricotta

1 tbsp freshly grated Parmesan

1 tbsp olive oil

salt and freshly ground pepper

freshly grated nutmeg

FOR THE LEMON BUTTER

175g (6oz) unsalted butter

½ garlic clove, crushed

100ml (3½fl oz) Vegetable Stock (see page 44)

zest and juice of 1 lemon, plus extra zest, to garnish

1 tbsp chopped fresh flatleaf parsley, plus leaves, to garnish

1 For the filling, heat the butter in a pan with the garlic and cumin seeds. When the butter is frothy and the spices are fragrant, add the spinach and cook over a low heat for 3–4 minutes until tender. Transfer the mixture to a bowl, cover, and chill thoroughly.

2 When chilled, add the ricotta and Parmesan, and stir until well combined. Season with salt, pepper, and nutmeg.

3 Roll out the pasta dough into four sheets (see page 43) and make and cook the ravioli (see steps 1–3, below).

4 When the ravioli are cooked and drained, place on a clean tea towel and pat off any excess moisture. Place the ravioli on a warmed plate, drizzle with olive oil, and keep warm while you prepare the lemon butter.

5 For the lemon butter, melt the butter with the garlic in a small pan over a medium heat, add the stock, and bring to the boil. Reduce the heat to low and simmer for 5–8 minutes. Add the lemon zest and juice, stir in, and season to taste.

6 Divide the ravioli between four serving plates. Pour a little lemon butter over the ravioli and serve garnished with a few strands of lemon zest, a sprinkling of chopped parsley, and a few parsley leaves.

Preparation & cooking time
1 hour, plus 1 hour for the stock, and 30 minutes for the pasta dough

Serves 4

Nutritional notes
kcalories 740; protein 18g; carbohydrate 49g; total fat 54g, of which saturated fat 31g; fibre 3g; sodium 343mg

MAKING & COOKING THE RAVIOLI

1 *Lay out the pasta sheets on a lightly floured work surface. Brush the pasta with water, then put small teaspoons of filling on to the pasta in rows, placing them about 5cm (2 inches) apart.*

2 *Cover with a second sheet of pasta and cut into squares with a pasta wheel or sharp knife. Press the edges together with your fingers, to ensure that they are well sealed. Place the ravioli on a floured tray.*

3 *Cook the ravioli in a pan of boiling, salted water. Cook for 2–3 minutes then, when they rise to the surface, lift them out and drain on a slotted spoon.*

PENNE WITH BROCCOLI & BROAD BEAN PESTO

It might seem fiddly peeling the broad beans to make this pesto, but using only the tender inner kernel results in extra vibrancy of colour and sweetness of flavour. This is a very fresh-tasting pesto, perfect for early summer.

INGREDIENTS

450g (1lb) broccoli, cut in small florets

450g (1lb) penne

150g (5½ oz) ripe cherry tomatoes, halved

salt and freshly ground pepper

freshly ground nutmeg

FOR THE PESTO

350g (12oz) broad beans, shelled

50g (1¾oz) fresh basil, plus a few leaves, to garnish

1 tbsp pine nuts

2 tbsp freshly grated Parmesan, plus shavings, to garnish

2 garlic cloves, peeled

100ml (3½fl oz) extra virgin olive oil

1 For the pesto, blanch the broad beans in boiling water for 1 minute, refresh in cold water, then drain and dry them.

2 Peel off the outer skins to reveal the green beans. Place the beans in a blender or food processor with all the pesto ingredients except the oil, and blend until finely chopped. With the motor still running, slowly drizzle in the oil until smooth and slightly runny. Season.

3 Blanch the broccoli in boiling, salted water for 3 minutes. Refresh in cold water; set aside.

4 Cook the penne in boiling, salted water according to packet instructions until al dente; drain. Return to the pan, season with salt, pepper, and nutmeg, and mix in the broccoli and tomatoes. Transfer to a serving dish, and add the pesto. Toss lightly and garnish with basil and Parmesan shavings.

Preparation & cooking time
30 minutes

Serves 4

Nutritional notes
kcalories 767; protein 27g; carbohydrate 96g; total fat 33g, of which saturated fat 6g; fibre 12g; sodium 181mg

LINGUINE WITH PORTABELLA MUSHROOMS

Juicy, grilled mushrooms make a deeply flavoursome sauce for pasta. Here, their flavour is intensified with a little red wine vinegar. You do not need to serve Parmesan with this dish, so it is a good choice for vegans, too.

INGREDIENTS

250g (9oz) Portabella (chestnut) mushrooms

6 tbsp extra virgin olive oil

500g (1lb 2oz) linguine

1 tbsp red wine vinegar

2 tbsp chopped mixed herbs (such as oregano, chives, mint, and thyme)

1 garlic clove, crushed

juice of ½ lemon

salt and freshly ground pepper

1 Trim the stems from the mushrooms and discard the stems. Wipe the mushrooms with a cloth to remove any dirt.

2 Brush both sides of the mushrooms liberally with half the olive oil. Grill the mushrooms, preferably on a griddle pan, or under a hot grill, for 5–8 minutes, turning them occasionally, until tender.

3 Meanwhile, cook the linguine in boiling, salted water according to packet instructions until al dente. Drain, then put back in the pan to keep warm. Toss in a little oil to prevent the pasta from sticking.

4 Remove the mushrooms from the grill, and cut them into 3mm (⅛ inch) slices. Put the mushrooms and any mushroom juices in a small bowl. Add the vinegar, remaining oil, herbs, garlic, and lemon juice to the mushrooms, mix together well, and season to taste.

5 Place the mushrooms in the pan with the pasta and toss together well. Serve in warmed, large, individual bowls.

Preparation & cooking time
30 minutes

Serves 4

Nutritional notes
kcalories 592; protein 16g; carbohydrate 94g; total fat 19g, of which saturated fat 2g; fibre 5g; sodium 114mg

TRENETTE WITH COURGETTES & SAFFRON

The courgettes in this sauce are stewed with classic Provençal ingredients, such as olive oil, saffron, fennel seeds, and garlic, to make a delicate, summery sauce. Be sure to use the best, fresh, firm courgettes.

INGREDIENTS

4 large courgettes, cut in half lengthways

6 tbsp olive oil

3 garlic cloves, crushed

½ tsp fennel seeds

good pinch saffron or ¼ tsp powdered saffron

200g (7oz) can chopped tomatoes

pinch granulated sugar

450g (1lb) trenette or other long, thin pasta

salt and freshly ground pepper

handful fresh basil, chopped, to serve

1 Scoop out the centre seeds from the courgettes with a teaspoon, then slice the courgettes into 5mm (¼ inch) thick slices to form small crescents.

2 Heat the oil in a frying pan, add the garlic, fennel seeds, and saffron, and fry over a medium heat for 30 seconds. Add the courgettes and stir well to coat them with the oil.

3 Reduce the heat and leave the courgettes to stew for about 12–15 minutes until they are soft and translucent. Add the tomatoes and cook for 5 minutes. Season with salt and pepper, and stir in the sugar.

4 Cook the trenette in boiling, salted water according to packet instructions until al dente. Drain, then toss in the vegetables. Adjust the seasoning and serve sprinkled with fresh basil.

Preparation & cooking time
45 minutes

Serves 4

Nutritional notes
kcalories 569; protein 16g; carbohydrate 89g; total fat 19g, of which saturated fat 3g; fibre 5g; sodium 123mg

SPAGHETTI WITH FENNEL, CHARD & PARMESAN

This simple sauce of lightly caramelized vegetables works well with a variety of pasta shapes, but here I have used it with spaghetti. You could also serve the vegetables as a dish on their own.

INGREDIENTS

1 fennel, with fronds

4 tbsp olive oil

1 onion, thinly sliced

300g (10½oz) Swiss chard, washed and roughly shredded

75g (2¼oz) sun-dried tomatoes

4 tbsp balsamic vinegar

100ml (3½fl oz) Vegetable Stock (see page 44)

450g (1lb) spaghetti

100g (3½oz) freshly grated Parmesan

salt and freshly ground pepper

freshly grated nutmeg

1 Remove the fronds from the fennel and slice it thinly. Reserve the fennel and fronds.

2 Heat half the oil in a large frying pan, add the onion and fennel, and sauté over a medium heat for 8–10 minutes until golden and soft.

3 Add the chard and sweat for a further 2–3 minutes until the chard just begins to wilt. Stir in the sun-dried tomatoes and balsamic vinegar.

4 Pour in the vegetable stock, raise the heat, and bring to the boil. Reduce the heat and simmer until the stock has evaporated and the chard is tender. Meanwhile, cook the spaghetti in boiling, salted water according to packet instructions until al dente. Drain, return to the pan, and keep warm.

5 When the chard is tender, add the cooked spaghetti to the pan with half the Parmesan. Toss lightly together and season with salt, pepper, and nutmeg.

6 Transfer to a serving bowl, scatter the fennel fronds on top, sprinkle with the remaining oil and Parmesan, and serve.

Preparation & cooking time
45 minutes, plus 1 hour for the stock

Serves 4

Nutritional notes
kcalories 734; protein 27g; carbohydrate 92g; total fat 31g, of which saturated fat 8g; fibre 6g; sodium 734mg

RED PEPPER TAGLIATELLE WITH CHILLI SAUCE

This spicy, homemade tagliatelle is surprisingly easy to make. Whizzed up in a food processor and then rolled out using a hand-cranked pasta machine, it can be ready to go in the cooking pot within just half an hour of beginning the preparations.

INGREDIENTS

FOR THE PASTA DOUGH

2 red peppers, halved and deseeded

1 small red chilli, deseeded and chopped

2 large eggs, plus 1 large egg yolk

1 tbsp olive oil

425g (15oz) strong plain flour, plus extra, to dust

1 tsp salt

FOR THE SAUCE

150ml (¼ pint) olive oil

2 garlic cloves, crushed

½ tsp red chilli oil

2 courgettes, sliced

1 red pepper, halved, deseeded, and quartered

2 small aubergines, sliced

1 red onion, cut in thin rings

6 oyster mushrooms

salt and freshly ground pepper

1 For the pasta dough, blend the peppers to a coarse purée in a blender or food processor. Add the chilli and blend. Add the eggs and oil and blend until smooth. Mix in the flour and salt until you have a firm dough. Cover and leave to rest for 30 minutes.

2 Knead the dough, roll it out into thin sheets, and cut in thin strips (see page 43).

3 For the sauce, mix together the olive oil, crushed garlic, chilli oil, and salt in a large bowl. Toss the vegetables in the mixture to coat them. Remove the vegetables from the oil and reserve the oil. Grill the vegetables on a medium to high heat for 5 minutes on each side until golden and tender. Return the vegetables to the oil.

4 Cook the tagliatelle in a pan of boiling, salted water for 2 minutes until al dente. Drain the pasta, then toss with the vegetables and oil, and season.

Preparation & cooking time
40 minutes, plus 30 minutes resting time

Serves 4

Nutritional notes
kcalories 897; protein 20g; carbohydrate 102g; total fat 49g, of which saturated fat 8g; fibre 8g; sodium 666mg

ASIAN POTSTICKERS

If you do not have the time to make the dough for this recipe, you can always buy a packet of wonton wrappers measuring 7cm (2¾ inches) square and use them instead. Serve with your favourite dipping sauce.

INGREDIENTS

150g (5½oz) plain flour, plus extra, to dust

110ml (3¾fl oz) boiling water

2 tbsp soy sauce

Chinese Dipping Sauce (see page 52) or a Thai sweet chilli sauce, to serve

FOR THE FILLING

4 tbsp vegetable oil

½ onion, finely chopped

2.5cm (1 inch) piece fresh root ginger, finely chopped

1 garlic clove, crushed

¼ tsp dried chilli flakes

150g (5½oz) shiitake mushrooms, chopped

75g (2¾oz) dried black beans, soaked overnight and cooked (see page 41)

50g (1¾oz) breadcrumbs

2 tbsp chopped fresh coriander

salt and freshly ground pepper

1 For the dough, place the flour in a large bowl. Gradually stir in the water until most of it is incorporated; add more water if the dough is too dry. Knead for 5–6 minutes until smooth. Return the dough to the bowl, cover with clingfilm, and leave to rest in a cool place for 30 minutes.

2 For the filling, heat half the oil in a frying pan and fry the onion, ginger, garlic, and chilli flakes for 1 minute over a medium heat. Raise the heat, add the mushrooms and cooked beans, and fry for 4 minutes. Add the breadcrumbs and coriander, mix well, season, then leave to cool.

3 Knead the dough with a little more flour. Roll into ropes 20cm (8 inches) long by 2cm (¾ inch) wide. Cut into 20 equal segments. Roll each one into 6cm (2½ inch) flat rounds. Place on a lightly floured tray.

4 Place 1 tablespoon of the filling in the centre of each round of dough. Moisten the edge with water and pinch together with your fingers to seal and form small pasties.

5 Heat the remaining oil in a large, non-stick pan until hot. Place the potstickers in the pan in one layer and fry them over a medium heat until they are lightly browned on one side.

6 Add 150ml (¼ pint) water and the soy sauce and cover. Raise the heat a little and cook for 10–12 minutes until the liquid is absorbed and the potstickers are crispy on one side.

7 Arrange the potstickers on a plate, crispy side up. Serve with the Chinese dipping sauce, or a Thai sweet chilli sauce.

Preparation & cooking time
2¼–2¾ hours, plus overnight soaking time

Serves 4

Nutritional notes
kcalories 392; protein 13g; carbohydrate 56g; total fat 14g, of which saturated fat 2g; fibre 3g; sodium 925mg

BAKED SWEET POTATO GNOCCHI WITH LEMON

Make sure that you buy the orange-fleshed sweet potatoes rather than the white ones to make these unusual gnocchi — not only is the colour more attractive, but the flavour is sweeter, too.

INGREDIENTS

450g (1lb) orange sweet potatoes
50g (1¼oz) freshly grated Parmesan, plus 2 tbsp extra, to serve
25g (1oz) butter
2 egg yolks
150g (5½oz) plain flour, plus extra, to dust
good pinch of cinnamon
salt and freshly ground pepper
pinch freshly grated nutmeg

FOR THE SAUCE

125ml (4fl oz) Vegetable Stock (see page 44)
125g (4½oz) butter
2 tbsp fresh coriander
zest and juice of ½ lemon

1 Bake the sweet potatoes whole for 1–1¼ hours until tender. When cool enough, peel, then mash them in a bowl while they are still warm. Add the Parmesan, butter, and egg yolks, and half the flour. Add the cinnamon, seasoning, and the nutmeg.

2 Turn the mixture on to a floured surface and knead in the remaining flour, a little at a time, to form a smooth dough. Roll into 2cm (¾ inch) thick ropes, then cut into 1cm (½ inch) lengths. Place on a floured tray and leave to dry for 1 hour.

3 Poach the gnocchi, a few at a time, in a pan of boiling, salted water for 4–5 minutes. When they rise to the surface, remove with a slotted spoon and drain. Season with salt, pepper, and nutmeg, and keep warm.

4 For the sauce, boil together the stock and butter, add the coriander and lemon zest and juice, and season. Arrange the gnocchi in a serving bowl and pour the sauce over them. Serve with Parmesan.

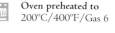

Oven preheated to 200°C/400°F/Gas 6

Preparation & cooking time 2½ hours, plus 1 hour for the stock

Serves 4

Nutritional notes kcalories 612; protein 14g; carbohydrate 53g; total fat 40g, of which saturated fat 25g; fibre 4g; sodium 622mg

OLIVE BREAD GNOCCHI

These are one of the easiest gnocchi to make and the breadcrumbs give them a lovely, light texture. They can be served with just a sprinkling of cheese, or with a tomato or red pepper sauce (see right) for a more substantial dish.

INGREDIENTS

450g (1lb) olive bread, made into breadcrumbs
350ml (12fl oz) milk
1 egg, beaten
125g (4½oz) freshly grated Parmesan
1 tsp salt
450g (1lb) flour, plus extra, to dust

FOR THE SAUCE

100g (3½oz) butter, plus extra, to grease
1 garlic clove, crushed
2 tbsp chopped fresh basil

1 Place the breadcrumbs in a bowl, then add the milk, egg, Parmesan, and salt. Add enough flour to make a thick dough, and knead for about 4–5 minutes until pliable. Turn out on to a floured work surface and knead until soft.

2 Roll the dough into 2.5cm (1 inch) thick ropes. Cut the ropes into 2cm (¾ inch) pieces. Roll each piece individually and place on a floured tray.

3 Drop the gnocchi, a few at a time, into a pan of boiling, salted water. Reduce the heat, then simmer for 2–3 minutes. When they rise to the surface, remove with a slotted spoon and place in a buttered serving dish.

4 For the sauce, heat the butter in a frying pan until foaming. Add the garlic and basil, then pour the sauce over the gnocchi.

Preparation & cooking time 25 minutes

Serves 4

Nutritional notes kcalories 1103; protein 40g; carbohydrate 152g; total fat 42g, of which saturated fat 24g; fibre 9g; sodium 2555mg

TRICOLOUR GNOCCHI WITH PEPPER SAUCE

Appropriately enough, these red, green, and white gnocchi share the colours of the Italian flag. Ricotta cheese makes them nice and light, while a warm red pepper and tomato vinaigrette replaces the usual butter and cheese sauces.

INGREDIENTS

250g (9oz) ricotta, drained and washed

200g (7oz) freshly grated Parmesan

100g (3½ oz) plain flour, plus extra, to dust

1 egg, plus 1 egg yolk, beaten together

200g (7oz) fresh spinach, stalks removed

1 tbsp sun-dried tomato paste or tomato purée

salt and freshly ground pepper

pinch freshly grated nutmeg

FOR THE SAUCE

1 red pepper, halved and deseeded

150ml (¼ pint) olive oil

1 garlic clove, crushed

pinch granulated sugar

4 tomatoes, skinned, deseeded, and chopped (see page 39)

bunch fresh basil, chopped, plus leaves, to garnish

1 Mix together the cheeses, flour, and eggs until well combined; season. Divide into three and place each portion in a separate bowl. Cover and chill for 1 hour.

2 Cook the spinach in its own water over a medium heat for 2 minutes until tender. Drain well, then chop finely. Add the spinach to one bowl of cheese mixture, the sun-dried tomato paste to the second, and leave the third plain. Season all three with salt, pepper, and nutmeg, and mix well.

3 With floured hands, roll each mixture into 2.5cm (1 inch) balls. Toss the balls in flour and set on a floured tray. Cook in a pan of boiling, salted water for 3–5 minutes until they rise to the surface. Remove with a slotted spoon and keep warm.

4 For the sauce, blend the red pepper in a blender or food processor until smooth, then strain. Heat the pepper in a pan over a low heat with the olive oil, garlic, and sugar for 5 minutes. Add the tomatoes and basil, and cook for 1 minute; season to taste.

5 Divide the gnocchi between four bowls, ensuring each has an equal amount of red, green, and white gnocchi. Coat with the warm pepper dressing and serve garnished with sprigs of fresh basil leaves.

Preparation & cooking time
1½ hours

Serves 4

Nutritional notes
kcalories 848; protein 33g; carbohydrate 28g; total fat 67g, of which saturated fat 21g; fibre 3g; sodium 860mg

STEWS & STIR-FRIES

These warming stews, stir-fries, casseroles, and curries are perfect for chilly days. A diverse range of ingredients is used in the recipes, and they often include rich sauces or wholesome toppings. They are simple to prepare and are therefore ideal both for entertaining and for more casual meals with friends. Some are robust dishes, slow-cooked to maximize the fragrances and flavours of the various ingredients, others are lighter fare, simply sautéed or stir-fried to seal in the flavours.

ROOT VEGETABLE PIE WITH POLENTA CRUST

KEY INGREDIENTS

Button onions are full of flavour and, left whole, lend texture and taste

Passata, pure, sieved tomatoes, is excellent in stews and sauces

Polenta is finely ground golden cornmeal, used often in Italian cooking

Baby carrots, Jerusalem artichokes, baby parsnips, and baby turnips provide contrasting colours and textures

Cannellini beans are good, all-purpose beans that are deliciously soft when cooked

On a cold winter's day, what could be more welcome than a warming root vegetable casserole? This one is cooked in a rich red wine and tomato sauce, and then baked with a golden polenta topping to make a satisfying pie. The polenta crust also makes an interesting topping for baked pasta dishes.

INGREDIENTS

400g (14oz) selection mixed root vegetables (such as baby carrots, Jerusalem artichokes, baby parsnips, baby turnips, and swede)
6 tbsp olive oil
1 onion, chopped
1 garlic clove, crushed
100g (3½oz) button onions, peeled
150g (5½oz) chestnut mushrooms, sliced
425g (15oz) can cannellini beans, drained
150ml (¼ pint) full-bodied red wine
600ml (1 pint) Dark Vegetable Stock (see page 44)
600ml (1 pint) tomato passata
salt and freshly ground pepper

FOR THE TOPPING

2 eggs
175ml (6fl oz) natural yogurt
150g (5½oz) Cheddar, grated
100g (3½oz) instant polenta
100g (3½oz) plain flour
1 tsp baking powder

1 Peel and dice the root vegetables, but only scrub the baby vegetables. Heat the oil in a large pan and fry the onion and garlic over a medium heat for 5 minutes until golden and soft. Add all the vegetables, button onions, and mushrooms, and fry them over a medium heat, stirring all the time, for 8 minutes until golden and slightly softened.

2 Add the beans, wine, stock, and passata. Bring to the boil, season, then transfer to a deep, 23cm (9 inch) ovenproof dish, and bake for 20–25 minutes.

3 Meanwhile, for the topping, whisk together the eggs and yogurt in a bowl. Stir in half the cheese, all the polenta, flour, and baking powder, and mix well. Remove the dish from the oven and spread the topping over it to make a thick crust. Sprinkle the remaining cheese over the top and bake for 25 minutes until golden.

Oven preheated to 190°C/375°F/Gas 5

Preparation & cooking time 1½ hours, plus 1 hour for the stock

Serves 4

Nutritional notes kcalories 771; protein 31g; carbohydrate 77g; total fat 37g, of which saturated fat 12g; fibre 11g; sodium 963mg

WINTER VEGETABLE ROOTATOUILLE

Ratatouille is one of those classic dishes that is usually regarded as sacred, but I like to experiment, and was delighted to find that ingredients with traditional Provençal flavours, such as garlic, olives, oregano, and tomatoes, make a perfect match for root vegetables.

INGREDIENTS

6 tbsp olive oil

250g (9oz) red potatoes, peeled and cut in 2.5cm (1 inch) wedges

250g (9oz) parsnips, sliced

200g (7oz) swede, cut in 2.5cm (1 inch) wedges

150g (5½oz) carrots, sliced

2 garlic cloves, crushed

50g (1¾oz) pitted black olives

200g (7oz) can tomatoes, drained and chopped

150ml (¼ pint) tomato passata

2 tsp chopped fresh oregano, or 1 tsp dried oregano

salt and freshly ground pepper

1 In a large casserole dish, heat the olive oil and sauté the root vegetables and garlic together for 2–3 minutes over a medium heat, stirring occasionally.

2 Add the olives and cook for a further 5 minutes, then add the tomatoes and passata.

3 Cover the dish, and transfer to the oven. Bake for 50 minutes until the vegetables are just cooked and coated in the sauce. Check the casserole from time to time and add a little water or stock if it becomes too dry. Add the oregano 5 minutes before the end of the cooking time, season, and stir.

Oven preheated to 190°C/375°F/Gas 5

Preparation & cooking time 1¼ hours

Serves 4

Nutritional notes kcalories 295; protein 4g; carbohydrate 28g; total fat 19g, of which saturated fat 3g; fibre 7g; sodium 427mg

ULTIMATE SHEPHERD'S PIE WITH CRUSHED POTATO

A pie, I am sure, that any shepherd would be proud of! What makes it special is its luxurious topping of buttery, crushed new potatoes with spring onions and parsley. Root vegetables in a light sauce are a delicious alternative to the traditional meat filling normally associated with this dish.

INGREDIENTS

150g (5½oz) parsnips, cut in 2.5cm (1 inch) pieces

150g (5½oz) celeriac, cut in 2.5cm (1 inch) pieces

2 carrots, cut in 2.5cm (1 inch) pieces

1 sweet potato, cut in 2.5cm (1 inch) pieces

150g (5½oz) Jerusalem artichoke, cut in 2.5cm (1 inch) pieces

150g (5½oz) baby onions

1 litre (1¾ pints) Vegetable Stock (see page 44)

50g (1¾oz) butter, plus extra, to grease

2 tbsp plain flour

300ml (½ pint) milk

1 tbsp Dijon mustard

salt and freshly ground pepper

FOR THE TOPPING

900g (2lb) waxy potatoes, washed and cut in equal-sized pieces

75g (2¾oz) unsalted butter

4 spring onions, finely chopped

2 tbsp roughly chopped fresh flatleaf parsley

1 For the topping, cook the potatoes in boiling, salted water for 20–25 minutes until tender. Drain, then crush them roughly with a fork. Add half the butter, the spring onions, and parsley. Season and mix well.

2 For the pie, simmer the vegetables in the stock for 15 minutes until tender. Drain, reserving 300ml (½ pint) stock, and keep the vegetables warm.

3 Heat the butter in a medium pan over a medium heat. Stir in the flour, then slowly add the milk. Heat until it boils and thickens. Reduce the heat and cook for 8–10 minutes. Add the reserved stock, season, and add the mustard. Mix in the vegetables.

4 Spoon the mixture into a greased, ovenproof dish and cover with the topping. Dot with the remaining butter. Bake for 20–25 minutes until piping hot and brown and crispy on top.

Oven preheated to 200°C/400°F/Gas 6

Preparation & cooking time 1¾ hours, plus 1 hour for the stock

Serves 6

Nutritional notes kcalories 403; protein 8g; carbohydrate 50g; total fat 20g, of which saturated fat 13g; fibre 7g; sodium 268mg

ASIAN STIR-FRY WITH COCONUT & LEMONGRASS

The refreshing citrus taste of lemongrass adds a delicate Oriental note to any dish. This simple stir-fry is enriched with coconut milk and ketjap manis, an Indonesian, aniseed-flavoured, sweet soy sauce. Serve it with fragrant Thai white rice.

INGREDIENTS

300g (10½oz) broccoli, cut in florets
1 corn on the cob, cut in 8 pieces
2.5cm (1 inch) piece fresh root ginger
50g (1¼oz) butter
2 tbsp sesame oil
1 garlic clove, crushed
¼ tsp turmeric
2 sticks lemongrass, finely shredded
2 green chillies, deseeded and thinly sliced
75g (2¾oz) sugar-snap peas
50g (1¼oz) beansprouts
2 carrots, sliced
2 spring onions, sliced
75g (2¾oz) oyster or shiitake mushrooms
400ml (14fl oz) can coconut milk
2 tbsp ketjap manis (Indonesian soy sauce)
125g (4½oz) firm tofu, cubed (optional)
salt and freshly ground pepper
coriander leaves, to garnish

1 Blanch the broccoli and corn on the cob for 5 minutes in separate pans of boiling water. Drain and set aside.

2 Finely chop the ginger. Heat the butter and sesame oil in a wok or deep-sided frying pan. When hot, add the garlic, ginger, and turmeric, and cook together for 30 seconds to release the fragrances into the oil.

3 Add the shredded lemongrass and the chillies, then stir in all the vegetables. Stir-fry for 4–5 minutes until the vegetables are cooked, but still crisp. Add the coconut milk, ketjap manis, and tofu, if using.

4 Stir to combine, then bring to the boil. Boil for 2 minutes, then adjust the seasoning to taste. Garnish with coriander leaves.

Preparation & cooking time
30 minutes

Serves 4

Nutritional notes
kcalories 392; protein 21g; carbohydrate 25g; total fat 25g, of which saturated fat 8g; fibre 4g; sodium 770mg

CAULIFLOWER & LENTIL PALAK

Lentils and cauliflower are both sadly misused in vegetarian cookery and are often over-cooked and under-seasoned. In India, these two simple ingredients are treated with respect. Combined with an aromatic spice paste and cooked gently, they make a fragrant and satisfying dish. Serve this palak with basmati rice.

INGREDIENTS

2.5cm (1 inch) piece fresh root ginger, peeled
2 garlic cloves, peeled
2 green chillies, deseeded
1 onion, chopped
125ml (4fl oz) natural yogurt
6 tbsp vegetable oil
4 cardamom pods, cracked
1 bay leaf
1 tsp ground cumin
¼ tsp turmeric
1 tsp ground coriander
1 large cauliflower, cut in florets
200g (7oz) brown lentils, cooked (see page 41)
200g (7oz) can chopped tomatoes
300ml (½ pint) Vegetable Stock (see page 44)
200g (7oz) fresh or frozen spinach
salt and freshly ground pepper

1 Purée the ginger, garlic, and chillies in a blender or food processor. Stir in half the onion and all the yogurt; set aside.

2 Heat half the oil in a large pan. Add the cardamom and bay leaf, and cook over a low heat for 30 seconds. Add the remaining onion and fry until lightly browned. Add the cumin, turmeric, and ground coriander. Cook for a further 10–12 minutes.

3 Add the cauliflower, lentils, and yogurt mixture, then the tomatoes, remaining oil, and stock. Cook over a low heat, stirring gently, for 10–12 minutes until the cauliflower is tender and the sauce has reduced. Chop the spinach and add 5 minutes before the end of cooking. Season before serving.

Preparation & cooking time
1 hour 10 minutes, plus 1 hour for the stock

Serves 4

Nutritional notes
kcalories 400; protein 21g; carbohydrate 36g; total fat 20g, of which saturated fat 3g; fibre 8g; sodium 232mg

PAUL'S RATATOUILLE NICOISE

Everybody knows and loves ratatouille, so what is different about mine? Heating the basil and oil together and adding them to the ratatouille at the end of its cooking time brings a freshness and vitality that I know you will enjoy.

INGREDIENTS

4 tbsp extra virgin olive oil

1 onion, finely chopped

4 garlic cloves, crushed

½ tbsp tomato purée

650g (1lb 7oz) ripe tomatoes, skinned, deseeded (see page 39), and quartered

½ tsp caster sugar

1 bouquet garni, comprising celery, leek, rosemary, thyme, ½ bay leaf, oregano, and basil (see page 39)

vegetable oil, for frying

1 large aubergine, cut in 2cm (¾ inch) dice

2 red peppers, halved, deseeded, and cut in 2cm (¾ inch) dice

1 green pepper, halved, deseeded, and cut in 2cm (¾ inch) dice

350g (12oz) courgettes, cut in 2cm (¾ inch) slices

12 fresh basil leaves, chopped

salt and freshly ground pepper

Oven preheated to
190°C/375°F/Gas 5

Preparation & cooking time
1¼ hours

Serves 4

Nutritional notes
kcalories 307; protein 5g;
carbohydrate 19g;
total fat 24g, of which
saturated fat 3g;
fibre 7g; sodium 128mg

1 Heat 2 tablespoons of the olive oil in a heavy-bottomed pan, add the onion and half the garlic, and sweat over a medium heat for 5 minutes until soft. Stir in the tomato purée, reduce the heat, and cook for 2–3 minutes. Stir in the tomatoes and sugar, and add the bouquet garni. Cook over a low heat for 10–15 minutes, stirring, until thickened.

2 In a large frying pan, heat 4 tablespoons of vegetable oil. Fry the aubergine over a medium heat for 5–10 minutes, stirring occasionally until golden. Add more oil if needed. Drain.

3 Heat a little more vegetable oil in the same pan and add the peppers. Fry over a low heat for 8–10 minutes, stirring, until tender, then drain. Finally, add a little more oil to the pan and fry the courgettes for about 2 minutes on either side until tender and golden. Drain in the colander.

4 Add the vegetables to the tomato mixture. Season lightly and transfer to a large, ovenproof dish. Cover and bake for about 10–15 minutes.

5 Heat the remaining olive oil in a small pan with the remaining garlic and the basil, and fry for a few seconds until the basil is wilted. Remove the ratatouille from the oven. Discard the bouquet garni, then stir in the garlic and basil oil. Adjust the seasoning and serve hot.

PUMPKIN, SWEET POTATO & BANANA CURRY

Although many vegetables would work well in this curry, I particularly like the contrast between the sweet vegetables, the banana, and the fiery sauce. The refreshing yogurt and coriander chutney takes seconds to prepare and makes a good accompaniment to other hot curries and spicy dishes. Serve this dish with the rice of your choice.

INGREDIENTS

2 tbsp vegetable oil
1 onion, finely chopped
1 garlic clove, crushed
2.5cm (1 inch) piece fresh root ginger, finely grated
½ tsp fenugreek seeds
1 stick lemongrass, finely chopped
4 tbsp Thai red curry paste
½ tsp turmeric
350g (12oz) pumpkin, peeled, deseeded, and cut in large cubes
300g (10½oz) sweet potato, peeled and cut in large cubes
300ml (½ pint) Vegetable Stock (see page 44)
300ml (½ pint) coconut milk
2 bananas, peeled and diced
salt and freshly ground pepper

FOR THE YOGURT CHUTNEY

150ml (¼ pint) natural yogurt
½ tsp mustard seeds
2 tbsp chopped fresh coriander, plus a few leaves, to garnish

1 Heat the oil in a large pan and fry the onion, garlic, ginger, and fenugreek over a low heat for about 5 minutes until the onion is softened. Stir in the lemongrass, curry paste, and turmeric.

2 Add the pumpkin and sweet potato, and stir to coat them in the spices. Leave to cook over a low heat for 2–3 minutes to allow the vegetables to absorb the flavours of the spices.

3 Pour in the vegetable stock and coconut milk. Bring to the boil, lower the heat, and simmer gently for 15–20 minutes until the vegetables are tender. Season, remove from the heat, then add the diced bananas.

4 For the chutney, blend together all the ingredients in a blender or food processor. When the curry is cooked, garnish it with a few fresh coriander leaves. Serve it with the yogurt chutney on the side.

Preparation & cooking time
50 minutes, plus 1 hour for the stock

Serves 4

Nutritional notes
kcalories 285; protein 6g; carbohydrate 41g; total fat 12g, of which saturated fat 2g; fibre 4g; sodium 549mg

WILD MUSHROOM STROGANOFF WITH SPATZELE

Spatzele, which means "little sparrows" in German, are tiny, dumpling-like noodles, a speciality of Alsace and Germany. They are convenient because they can be poached a day or two in advance, then stored in the refrigerator, and heated in butter at the last moment. Here, spinach-flavoured spatzele are served in elegant little mounds to accompany a rich, Russian-inspired mushroom stew.

INGREDIENTS

2 tbsp olive oil
1 tbsp Hungarian paprika
550g (1lb 4oz) selection mixed wild mushrooms, well cleaned
2 shallots, finely chopped
3 tbsp white wine vinegar
6 tbsp dry white wine
300ml (½ pint) double cream
150ml (¼ pint) Brown Mushroom Stock (see page 44)
1 tbsp cocktail gherkins, thinly shredded
1 tsp Dijon mustard

FOR THE SPATZELE

150g (5½oz) spinach, blanched and finely chopped
5 eggs, lightly beaten
350g (12oz) plain flour
¼ tsp baking powder
50g (1¾oz) butter
salt and freshly ground pepper
freshly grated nutmeg

1 For the spatzele, blend together the spinach, eggs, and 125ml (4fl oz) water in a blender or food processor. Sift the flour into a bowl, add the baking powder, and season with salt, pepper, and nutmeg. Add the spinach mixture.

2 See Steps 1–3 below for how to make the spatzele. When cooked, refresh in iced water. Use immediately, or toss in oil and keep in the refrigerator until needed.

3 For the stroganoff, heat the oil in a sauté pan. Place half the paprika on a large plate and dust the mushrooms in it, then sprinkle them with salt. Fry the seasoned mushrooms over a medium heat for 1 minute. Add the shallots and fry for a further minute. Lift out the mushrooms and keep warm.

4 Pour the vinegar and wine into the pan containing the shallots and bring to the boil. Stir in the cream and reduce the sauce by half. Add the stock, then reduce the sauce until thick enough to coat the back of a spoon. Add the gherkins and stir in the mustard and remaining paprika. Stir in the mushrooms and season.

5 Heat the butter in a large pan and fry the spatzele for 2 minutes until golden. Season with salt, pepper, and nutmeg, then place in dariole moulds. Turn the spatzele out on to serving plates. Serve hot with the stroganoff.

Preparation & cooking time
1 hour, plus 1 hour for the stock

Serves 4

Nutritional notes
kcalories 953; protein 24g; carbohydrate 75g; total fat 63g, of which saturated fat 33g; fibre 6g; sodium 553mg

MAKING THE SPATZELE

1 *Gently beat together the ingredients (see step 1, above) to form a smooth, very thick batter, almost dough-like in texture.*

2 *Place a colander over a pan of boiling, salted water. Pour one-third of the batter in at a time. Press the batter through the holes with a spatula.*

3 *When the spatzele float to the surface, reduce the heat. Cook for 3–4 minutes until they swell and become fluffy. Remove with a slotted spoon.*

HUNGARIAN STEW WITH CARAWAY DUMPLINGS

Hungarian cuisine is full of hearty stews, spiced with pungent, sweet paprika and topped with light, fluffy dumplings. This combination works well for vegetarians too, especially now that vegetarian suet is so easy to obtain. You can steam the dumplings on top of the casserole for the last ten minutes of cooking instead of poaching them, if you prefer.

INGREDIENTS

4 tbsp olive oil

1 garlic clove, crushed

100g (3½oz) button onions

1 celery stick, sliced

1 carrot, sliced

½ swede, cut in large dice

1 kohlrabi, cut in large dice

1 medium parsnip, sliced

½ medium cauliflower, cut in florets

1 potato, cut in large dice

1 tsp caraway seeds

1 tbsp Hungarian paprika

1 tbsp tomato purée

2 tbsp plain flour

300ml (½ pint) white wine

600ml (1 pint) Vegetable Stock (see page 44)

salt and freshly ground pepper

3 tbsp chopped fresh parsley, to garnish

FOR THE DUMPLINGS

50g (1¾oz) rye flour

50g (1¾oz) self-raising flour

40g (1½oz) vegetarian suet

pinch caraway seeds

1 tsp grated fresh horseradish

1 Heat the olive oil in a large, heavy-bottomed pan and fry the garlic, onions, and celery over a medium heat for 4–5 minutes until golden. Add the remaining vegetables and fry for 2 minutes until browned, then add the caraway seeds, paprika, and tomato purée. Cook for a further 3 minutes.

2 Add the flour and cook, stirring, for 2–3 minutes. Gradually pour in the wine and stock, stirring. Season and bring to the boil. Lower the heat and simmer for 15–20 minutes until tender.

3 For the dumplings, place the flours in a bowl with a little salt and pepper. Stir in the suet, caraway seeds, and horseradish. Add 4 tablespoons of water, or enough to bind the mixture into a smooth, firm dough. Roll the dough into 12 separate 2.5cm (1 inch) balls.

4 Poach the dumplings in a pan of boiling, salted water for 10 minutes until light and fluffy. Place on the casserole to serve, and sprinkle with the parsley.

Preparation & cooking time
1 hour 10 minutes, plus 1 hour for the stock

Serves 4

Nutritional notes
kcalories 501; protein 10g; carbohydrate 58g; total fat 22g, of which saturated fat 6g; fibre 9g; sodium 202mg

Pinto Bean, Aubergine & Tahini Moussaka

For me, aubergines and sesame have a great affinity. In this recipe for a rich, vegetarian version of this Greek dish, I infuse a classic white sauce with tahini, a sesame seed paste: it gives a wonderful, characteristic nutty flavour.

INGREDIENTS

150g (5½oz) dried pinto beans, soaked overnight and cooked (see page 41)

6 tbsp vegetable oil

1 onion, chopped

1 garlic clove, crushed

½ tsp ground cumin

2 tsp chopped fresh thyme or 1 tsp dried thyme

200g (7oz) can chopped tomatoes

1 tbsp tomato purée

2 large aubergines, sliced

salt and freshly ground pepper

FOR THE SAUCE

2 garlic cloves, peeled, but left whole

300ml (½ pint) milk

25g (1oz) butter

25g (1oz) flour

1 tbsp tahini (sesame seed paste)

1 egg, beaten

1 For the sauce, place the garlic cloves in a small pan with the milk. Cook over a low heat for about 20 minutes until the garlic is very soft. Blend the milk and garlic in a blender; set aside.

2 For the moussaka, drain the pinto beans, reserving any cooking liquor. Heat 2 tablespoons of the oil in a large pan and sweat the onion and garlic over a medium heat for 5 minutes until golden. Add the cooked pinto beans, cumin, thyme, chopped tomatoes, and tomato purée. Stir in the reserved cooking liquor from the beans and simmer for 20–25 minutes until the sauce has thickened. Season.

3 Heat the remaining oil in a large frying pan and fry the aubergines over a medium heat for 5 minutes on each side until golden. Remove and drain the excess oil on kitchen paper.

4 Arrange a layer of aubergines in the base of an ovenproof dish. Cover them with half the pinto beans, another layer of aubergines, the remaining beans, and a final layer of aubergines.

5 For the sauce, melt the butter in a small pan, stir in the flour to make a roux, and cook for 1 minute. Gradually stir in the garlic-infused milk and bring to the boil, stirring until the sauce thickens. Stir in the tahini paste and beat in the egg. Cook for 2–3 more minutes, stirring. Season to taste.

6 Spoon the sauce over the aubergines, to cover. Bake for 30–35 minutes until the topping is golden and bubbling.

Oven preheated to 200°C/400°F/Gas 6

Preparation & cooking time 3–3½ hours, plus overnight soaking time

Serves 4

Nutritional notes kcalories 445; protein 15g; carbohydrate 37g; total fat 28g, of which saturated fat 8g; fibre 10g; sodium 259mg

RICE & GRAINS

RICE AND GRAINS have traditionally provided the staple diets for people all around the world, and they are particularly important sources of nutrients for vegetarians. This section includes recipes that are traditional favourites in countries as far apart as Italy and Indonesia. I have included timeless classics such as paella and risotto and given them a new twist by fusing Eastern and Western flavours. I have also combined rice and grains with pulses to produce dishes that are packed with goodness.

MARDI GRAS JAMBALAYA

KEY INGREDIENTS

Thyme and bay leaves combine to impart a subtle flavour to stews

Arborio rice is the Italian risotto rice, but it can be used in any dish that calls for rice with a creamy texture

Celery, green pepper, and onion provide an excellent base for many stews, stocks, and sauces because they all have such strong flavours

Okra and baby corn are typical ingredients in Creole cooking

Red kidney beans are full of protein and bring a splash of colour to many dishes

This all-vegetable version of Louisiana's dazzling, famous Creole rice dish captures the colour and excitement of the New Orleans great, annual Mardi Gras festival.

INGREDIENTS

3 tbsp sunflower or olive oil
2 celery sticks, thinly sliced
1 green pepper, diced
1 onion, chopped
2 garlic cloves, crushed
1 large bay leaf
2 sprigs fresh thyme
1 litre (1¾ pints) Vegetable Stock (see page 44)
150g (5½oz) fresh okra
425g (15oz) can chopped tomatoes
100g (3½oz) baby corn
150g (5½oz) peeled squash or pumpkin, cut in 2cm (¾ inch) cubes
250g (9oz) arborio rice
425g (15oz) can red kidney beans, washed and drained
2 tbsp chopped fresh parsley
salt and freshly ground pepper
pinch cayenne pepper

1 Heat a large, heavy-bottomed pan over a medium heat. Add the oil and fry the celery, pepper, onion, and garlic for 7 minutes until lightly browned. Add the bay leaf and thyme and fry for a further 2 minutes. Add the stock, stir well, and bring to the boil.

2 Meanwhile, trim off the tops of the okra stems. Add the okra, tomatoes, baby corn, and squash to the pan, reduce the heat, and simmer for 5 minutes, then stir in the rice.

3 Season with salt, pepper, and cayenne pepper, to taste. Bring back to the boil, then reduce the heat to low, and simmer gently for 20 minutes, stirring occasionally.

4 Stir in the beans and parsley, and cook for 5 minutes more. When the rice is done, check the seasoning. Serve hot.

Preparation & cooking time
55 minutes, plus 1 hour for the stock

Serves 4

Nutritional notes
kcalories 455; protein 14g; carbohydrate 79g; total fat 12g, of which saturated fat 2g; fibre 9g; sodium 443mg

NASI GORENG

Perfect for a quick, satisfying snack, this spicy, Indonesian fried rice dish can be served with whatever garnishes you have to hand. Try cucumber, roasted peanuts, or chopped, fresh coriander. You can buy plum sauce from most supermarkets these days.

INGREDIENTS

FOR THE RICE

4 tbsp vegetable oil

1 onion, finely chopped

1 garlic clove, crushed

100g (3½oz) white cabbage, finely shredded

200g (7oz) long-grain rice, boiled

1 red chilli, deseeded and shredded

50g (1¼oz) cooked peas

2 tbsp ketjap manis (Indonesian soy sauce)

4 eggs

FOR THE CHILLI SAMBAL

4 tbsp vegetable oil

5cm (2 inch) piece fresh root ginger, grated

4 tomatoes, chopped

2 red chillies, deseeded and chopped

TO SERVE

1 banana, sliced

4 spring onions, sliced

plum sauce

1 For the chilli sambal, blend together all the ingredients in a blender or food processor to form a smooth paste.

2 For the rice, heat the oil in a wok, over a medium heat. Add the onion and garlic, and fry for 5 minutes. Add the cabbage and stir-fry for 1–2 minutes. Stir in the chilli sambal and mix well.

3 Continue to stir-fry for 1 minute. Increase the heat and add the cooked rice and chilli. Stir-fry for 2–3 minutes to heat the rice through. Stir in the peas and ketjap manis, and heat for a further minute. Keep warm.

4 Fry the eggs. Pile the rice on to four serving plates, top with the banana, and set one egg on each portion. Garnish with the spring onions. Spoon the plum sauce around to serve.

Preparation & cooking time
50 minutes

Serves 4

Nutritional notes
kcalories 518; protein 7g; carbohydrate 71g; total fat 25g, of which saturated fat 3g; fibre 3g; sodium 457mg

THAI-INSPIRED RISOTTO WITH PUMPKIN

This is one of the most successful East-West hybrids I have come across. It combines the classic Italian method of cooking a risotto with fragrant Thai flavourings, such as lemongrass, coconut milk, and coriander. In keeping with the Oriental theme, the cooked risotto is sprinkled with grated coconut instead of Parmesan.

INGREDIENTS

40g (1½oz) butter

1 onion, chopped

1 garlic clove, crushed

1 stick lemongrass, thinly sliced

1 red chilli, deseeded and chopped

½ tsp curry powder

2.5cm (1 inch) piece fresh root ginger, chopped

350g (12oz) pumpkin, peeled and cut in 1cm (½ inch) pieces

350g (12oz) arborio rice

100ml (3½fl oz) dry white wine

700ml (1¼ pints) Vegetable Stock (see page 44)

150ml (¼ pint) coconut milk

1 tbsp chopped fresh mint

1 tbsp chopped fresh coriander

salt and freshly ground pepper

grated coconut, to serve

1 Melt the butter in a large, heavy-bottomed pan. Add the onion, garlic, lemongrass, chilli, curry powder, and ginger, and cook, stirring, over a low heat for 5 minutes. Add the pumpkin and rice, and cook for 1 minute more. Pour in the wine and a ladleful of stock and cook, stirring, until the liquid is absorbed.

2 Keep adding the stock, a ladleful at a time, stirring continuously, until the rice is tender, but al dente, about 25 minutes. Towards the end of cooking, add the stock in smaller quantities and check frequently to see if the rice is cooked.

3 Add the coconut milk, mint, and coriander. Remove from the heat, season, and sprinkle with grated coconut to serve.

Preparation & cooking time
50 minutes, plus 1 hour for the stock

Serves 4

Nutritional notes
kcalories 448; protein 8g; carbohydrate 83g; total fat 12g, of which saturated fat 6g; fibre 2g; sodium 223mg

COCONUT RICE WITH ALMONDS & RAISINS

The rice in this dish gets its vivid colour from plenty of ground turmeric, which also adds a subtle flavour. It makes an attractive and tasty accompaniment to Indian and other Asian dishes.

INGREDIENTS

350ml (12fl oz) Vegetable Stock (see page 44)

300ml (½ pint) coconut milk

2 tbsp turmeric, mixed to a paste with 2 tbsp cold water

1 stick lemongrass, braised (see page 40)

350g (12oz) long-grain rice

TO SERVE

2 tbsp toasted, flaked almonds

1 green chilli, deseeded and very thinly sliced

2 tbsp raisins, soaked in cold water overnight

1 Combine the vegetable stock and coconut milk in a pan and bring to the boil, then reduce the heat to low and simmer. Stir in the turmeric paste, lemongrass, and rice, and stir well. Cover and simmer for 15 minutes until all the water has been absorbed. Remove from the heat and leave to rest, covered, for 2–3 minutes. Discard the lemongrass.

2 Transfer to a serving dish and sprinkle the almonds, chilli, and raisins over the top to serve.

Preparation & cooking time
30 minutes, plus 1 hour for the stock, plus overnight soaking for the raisins

Serves 4

Nutritional notes
kcalories 440; protein 9g; carbohydrate 90g; total fat 8g, of which saturated fat 1g; fibre 1g; sodium 98mg

VEGETARIAN PAELLA

In Spain, paella is cooked outdoors, over a wood fire. In less sunny climates you might have to abandon authenticity and retreat indoors to prepare this dish. The important thing is to use a good olive oil, genuine saffron, and short-grain rice. If you cannot get Spanish rice, use arborio rice instead.

INGREDIENTS

150ml (¼ pint) Vegetable Stock (see page 44), plus more if needed

½ tsp saffron

50g (1¾oz) peas

1 tbsp olive oil

1 onion, finely chopped

2 garlic cloves, crushed

2 Jerusalem artichokes, diced

1 aubergine, diced

3 peppers (1 red, 1 yellow, 1 green), halved, deseeded, and chopped

2 celery sticks, sliced

1 tsp Spanish paprika

50g (1¾oz) Spanish short-grain rice

6 tbsp dry white wine

425g (15oz) can chopped tomatoes

50g (1¾oz) French beans, cooked

2 tbsp pitted black olives

flatleaf parsley, to garnish

lemon wedges, to serve

1 Put 150ml (¼ pint) vegetable stock and the saffron in a large pan and bring to the boil, then remove from the heat and set aside. In a separate pan, boil the peas for about 5 minutes until tender.

2 Heat the oil in a large pan and fry the onion and garlic for 5 minutes over a medium heat until golden. Add the artichokes, aubergine, peppers, celery, paprika, and rice, and stir to coat in the oil. Cook for 2–3 minutes, stirring occasionally, until the rice becomes transparent.

3 Pour in the white wine and saffron-infused stock. Stir in the chopped tomatoes, reduce the heat, and cook for 20 minutes until tender. Add more stock if the rice becomes too dry. Stir in the French beans, olives, and peas. Garnish with parsley and place the lemon wedges on the side.

Preparation & cooking time
1 hour, plus 1 hour for the stock

Serves 4

Nutritional notes
kcalories 199; protein 6g; carbohydrate 32g; total fat 5g, of which saturated fat 1g; fibre 8g; sodium 130mg

LEMON COUSCOUS & CHERMOULA MUSHROOMS

The Moroccan spice mix "chermoula" gives the mushrooms a tantalizing aroma as they cook. Lemon pepper — finely ground, dried lemon zest — is a useful ingredient for flavouring grains and other bland foods. I first experienced lemon pepper on my travels in the Caribbean.

INGREDIENTS

3 tbsp vegetable oil

1 onion, chopped

2 garlic cloves, crushed

1 tsp cumin seeds

½ tsp dried chilli flakes

200g (7oz) chestnut mushrooms, halved

6 flat mushrooms, thickly sliced

1 tsp harissa paste

425g (15oz) can chopped tomatoes

2 tbsp finely chopped fresh coriander

FOR THE COUSCOUS

200g (7oz) couscous

250ml (9fl oz) Vegetable Stock (see page 44), boiling

juice of ½ lemon

1 tbsp Lemon Pepper (see page 45)

salt and freshly ground pepper

1 Place the couscous in a bowl with the vegetable stock and lemon juice, and cover. Leave for 5 minutes until the couscous has swollen. Fluff it up with a fork, cover again, and leave for 5 more minutes. Add the lemon pepper, season to taste with salt and pepper, and keep warm.

2 Heat the oil in a pan and fry the onion and garlic over a medium heat for 5 minutes. Add the cumin and chilli and cook for a few seconds before adding the mushrooms and harissa. Fry for 3 minutes, then add the tomatoes. Bring to the boil, reduce the heat, and simmer for 8–10 minutes. Stir in the chopped coriander. Serve the lemon couscous topped with the mushroom mixture.

Preparation & cooking time
30 minutes, plus 1 hour for the stock

Serves 4

Nutritional notes
kcalories 237; protein 7g; carbohydrate 33g; total fat 10g, of which saturated fat 1g; fibre 2g; sodium 162mg

TOASTED MILLET & CUMIN VEGETABLES

I like to use millet rather than the more familiar couscous in this recipe. Its wonderful, nutty flavour and crunchy texture make it a good partner for the roasted root vegetables. You can of course substitute couscous if you prefer. I sometimes top the vegetables with a little firm, diced goat's cheese for a tasty variation.

INGREDIENTS

4 small parsnips, halved lengthways

4 carrots, halved lengthways

8 new potatoes, quartered

1 sweet potato, cut in wedges, lengthways

1 leek, cut in 1cm (½ inch) slices

4 small baby beetroots, boiled and halved

FOR THE MARINADE

200ml (7fl oz) olive oil

2 bay leaves

2 garlic cloves, crushed

2 tbsp balsamic vinegar

1 tbsp ground cumin

50g (1¾oz) raisins, soaked overnight

4 tbsp chopped fresh coriander, plus leaves, to garnish

FOR THE MILLET

275g (9½oz) millet

1 garlic clove, crushed

¼ tsp ground cumin

600ml (1 pint) Vegetable Stock (see page 44)

salt and freshly ground pepper

1 Combine all the vegetables, except the beetroot, in a large bowl and add all the marinade ingredients. Toss the vegetables and marinade ingredients together well and leave to marinate for 1 hour.

2 Arrange the vegetables with the beetroot in a single layer in a shallow roasting tin. Roast for 25–30 minutes until lightly browned. Reduce the heat to 170°C/325°F/Gas 3, cover the tin, and cook for a further 30 minutes until the vegetables are firm outside, but soft inside.

3 Dry fry the millet in a large, non-stick frying pan over a medium heat for 5 minutes until toasted. Add the garlic and cumin. Meanwhile, bring the stock to the boil in a separate pan, then add the millet. Season lightly and cover with a lid. Reduce the heat and simmer for about 25 minutes until all the liquid has evaporated and the millet is tender and fluffy.

4 To serve, arrange a mound of millet on each serving plate, pile the roasted vegetables on top, and pour the roasting juices left in the pan over the vegetables. Garnish with coriander.

Oven preheated to 220°C/425°F/Gas 7

Preparation & cooking time
2 hours, plus 1 hour for the stock, plus 1 hour marinating time, plus overnight soaking for the raisins

Serves 4

Nutritional notes
kcalories 990; protein 11g; carbohydrate 118g; total fat 54g, of which saturated fat 8g; fibre 12g; sodium 233mg

SUCCOTASH PUDDING

Succotash is a traditional Native American dish made with corn and beans. This baked version contains a double dose of corn — sweetcorn kernels and cornmeal — plus red peppers and tomatoes for a colourful, savoury pudding.

INGREDIENTS

125g (4½oz) butter, plus extra, to grease

1 onion, finely chopped

1 garlic clove, crushed

200g (7oz) frozen or canned sweetcorn

3 tomatoes, skinned, deseeded, and chopped (see page 39)

1 red pepper, halved, deseeded, and diced

75g (2¾oz) French or broad beans, cooked

¼ tsp paprika

75g (2¾oz) cornmeal

salt and freshly ground pepper

1 Heat 25g (1oz) of the butter in a pan, add the onion and garlic, and sweat for 5 minutes over a medium heat until soft. Transfer to a bowl, and add all the remaining ingredients, except the cornmeal and remaining butter. Mix well, add the cornmeal, and season.

2 Butter a shallow, 1.2 litre (2 pint) casserole dish. Melt the remaining butter over a low heat and pour it over the cornmeal mixture. Mix again. Spoon into the casserole dish, and bake for 1 hour until puffed and golden.

Oven preheated to 160°C/325°F/Gas 3

Preparation & cooking time
1½ hours

Serves 4

Nutritional notes
kcalories 254; protein 6g; carbohydrate 36g; total fat 10g, of which saturated fat 6g; fibre 4g; sodium 317mg

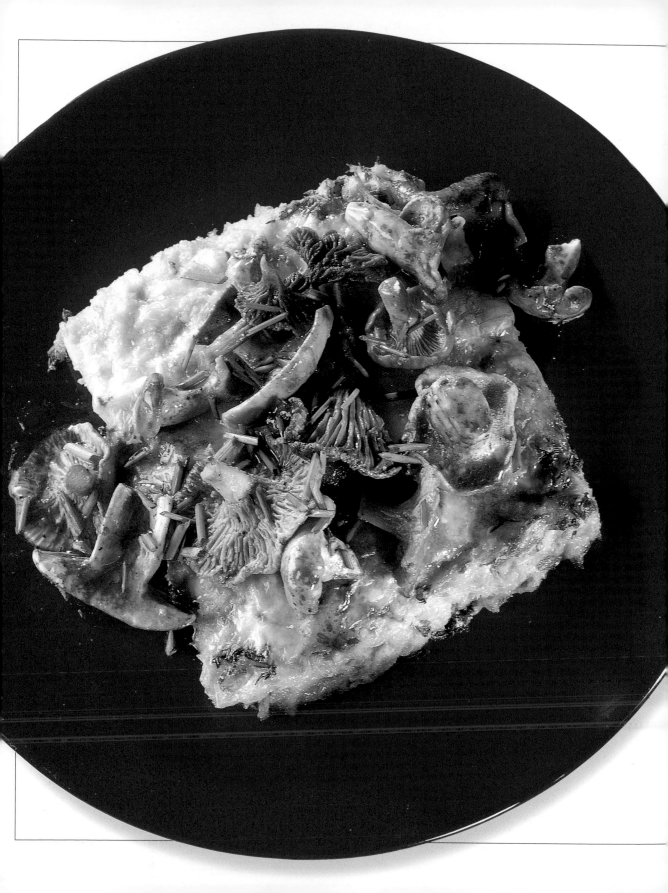

POLENTA VERDE WITH WILD MUSHROOMS

This green polenta gets its colour from the savoy cabbage, but you could use fresh spinach instead. The polenta squares or rounds can be prepared well in advance and kept in the refrigerator for up to two days, then baked just before serving.

INGREDIENTS

FOR THE POLENTA

50g (1¾oz) butter, plus extra, to grease, and to brush

1 garlic clove, crushed

½ savoy cabbage, shredded

85g (3oz) quick-cook polenta

25g (1oz) freshly grated Parmesan

½ tsp chopped fresh thyme

1 egg yolk, beaten

50g (1¾oz) Fontina, finely grated

salt and freshly ground pepper

FOR THE MUSHROOMS

50g (1¾oz) butter

100g (3½oz) mixed wild mushrooms

1 tbsp balsamic vinegar

2 tbsp chopped fresh chives, to garnish

1 Melt the butter in a large pan, add the garlic and cabbage, and cook over a low heat for 12–15 minutes, stirring all the time until the cabbage is soft.

2 Bring 700ml (1¼ pints) of water to the boil and cook the polenta (see step 1, below). When the polenta is cooked, remove from the heat, stir in the cabbage mixture, then add the Parmesan, thyme, and egg yolk, and stir well. Leave the polenta to set (see step 2, below).

3 Cover the polenta with clingfilm and place in the refrigerator for at least 4 hours, or preferably overnight, until set and firm to the touch. When set, turn out and cut (see step 3, below).

4 Lightly grease a baking sheet and transfer the portions of polenta on to the baking sheet. Brush the polenta with melted butter and sprinkle with the Fontina. Bake for 25–30 minutes until golden and sizzling.

5 Meanwhile, for the mushrooms, heat the butter in a large frying pan and sauté the wild mushrooms over a high heat for 5–8 minutes until cooked. Season, then add the balsamic vinegar. Cook for 2–3 minutes more, still over a high heat, stirring gently.

6 To serve, place a portion of polenta on each of six serving dishes, top with a mound of the wild mushrooms, and garnish with chopped chives.

Oven preheated to 200°C/400°F/Gas 6

Preparation & cooking time 1¼ hours, plus 4 hours or overnight to set

Serves 6

Nutritional notes kcalories 248; protein 8g; carbohydrate 12g; total fat 19g, of which saturated fat 12g; fibre 2g; sodium 325mg

PREPARING THE POLENTA

1 *Add the polenta to the pan of boiling, salted water, stirring continuously. Season and cook over a medium heat, stirring all the time, for 8–10 minutes until smooth and thick in consistency.*

2 *Transfer the mixture to a shallow baking sheet lined with clingfilm, and spread it out evenly with a spatula or palette knife, pressing down lightly as you spread.*

3 *Turn the chilled polenta out on to a clean work surface. Cut out six 10cm (4 inch) squares with a knife, or six 9–10cm (3¼–4 inch) rounds with a pastry cutter.*

STUFFED VEGETABLES

THESE RECIPES DEMONSTRATE how to add an extra dimension to vegetables as varied as the humble potato, the versatile pepper, and the more unusual gem squash. Nature has provided many vegetables complete with the perfect cooking vessel: their own shells. Stuffed vegetables not only look spectacular; the stuffings also retain their flavour and moisture when they are encased in succulent roast flesh. Small, stuffed vegetables make pretty starters, while larger ones, or larger servings, make ideal main dishes.

GREEK BABY VEGETABLES WITH ORZO

KEY INGREDIENTS

Mushrooms are full of flavour and texture

Orzo, a tiny pasta shaped like barley, is perfect for stuffings

Aubergine, courgette, and red pepper are widely used in Greek cookery

Mint has a fresh, light flavour

Feta is a soft, fresh Greek cheese with a sharp, tangy taste

Raisins are sweet and combine perfectly with salty feta

Stuffed vegetables are frequently offered as part of a meze (selection of snacks) in Greece, but a large selection of mixed, stuffed vegetables makes a splendid main course. You can serve them hot, but the Greek way is to serve them at room temperature. Orzo is a rice-shaped pasta, but rice would work equally well in the filling.

INGREDIENTS

4 tomatoes, halved
4 baby peppers
4 baby aubergines
4 small courgettes
4 button mushrooms, stalks removed
125ml (4fl oz) vegetable oil
salt and freshly ground pepper

FOR THE STUFFING

115g (4oz) feta, diced
100g (3½oz) orzo pasta, cooked
½ tbsp ground cumin
½ tbsp ground coriander
1½ tbsp raisins, soaked in water
1½ tbsp peanuts, toasted
1 tbsp chopped fresh mint
½ small onion, chopped

FOR THE SAUCE

100ml (3½ fl oz) extra virgin olive oil
½ tbsp chopped fresh flatleaf parsley
1 tbsp chopped fresh oregano
2 garlic cloves, crushed
juice of 1 lemon

1 Slice off the tomato tops and discard the tops. Scoop out the seeds. Cut the tops off the peppers and deseed them. Reserve the tops. Place all the vegetables except the tomatoes on the baking sheet with the pepper tops and brush with oil. Season and roast for 15 minutes; leave to cool.

2 Cut a small, horizontal slice off the top of each aubergine and courgette, and scoop out the centre. Mix half the feta with the other stuffing ingredients and the scooped out flesh from the vegetables. Fill all the vegetables with this mixture.

3 Place the vegetables and the tomatoes on the baking sheet, season, then bake for 5 minutes.

4 Blend together the sauce ingredients and 6 tablespoons of water. Replace the pepper tops. Place the vegetables on a plate, scatter the remaining feta around, and drizzle with the sauce.

Oven preheated to 200°C/400°F/Gas 6

Preparation & cooking time 45 minutes, plus 2 hours soaking time

Serves 4

Nutritional notes kcalories 712; protein 10g; carbohydrate 23g; total fat 66g, of which saturated fat 12g; fibre 6g; sodium 535mg

GEM SQUASH WITH TOFU

Tofu is often dismissed as bland and boring, but the great thing about it is that it absorbs the flavours of other ingredients — here an Italian-inspired mixture of sun-dried tomatoes, black olives, and thyme. Gem squash are perfect for single servings, but you could use two butternut squash, halved, instead.

INGREDIENTS

4 gem squash
1 tbsp olive oil
1 garlic clove, crushed
25g (1oz) sun-dried tomatoes
25g (1oz) pitted black olives, chopped
50g (1¾oz) fresh breadcrumbs
1 egg, beaten
2 tsp fresh thyme leaves, plus sprigs fresh thyme, to garnish
100g (3½oz) firm tofu, cubed
salt and freshly ground pepper

1 Bring a large pan of lightly salted water to the boil and blanch the squash whole for 10 minutes until tender. Drain them and set aside.

2 Heat the oil in a frying pan, add the garlic and sun-dried tomatoes, and sweat on a medium heat for 5 minutes until softened. Transfer to a bowl, then add the olives, breadcrumbs, egg, thyme leaves, and tofu. Stir until well combined with the garlic and tomatoes. Season to taste, then leave to cool.

3 Slice the top from each squash and carefully scoop out the seeds with a metal spoon; discard the seeds. Fill each squash with the tofu and thyme stuffing.

4 Turn the grill on to a low heat. Place the gem squash under the grill (without the tops) to cook slowly for 25–30 minutes until tender and heated through. Serve hot, with or without the tops, garnished with sprigs of fresh thyme on top.

Preparation & cooking time
1 hour

Serves 4

Nutritional notes
kcalories 221; protein 8g; carbohydrate 27g; total fat 10g, of which saturated fat 2g; fibre 4g; sodium 427mg

TOMATOES WITH GOAT'S CHEESE PESTO

Try to get well-flavoured, firm, ripe tomatoes for this dish. You could use cherry tomatoes and serve them as canapés, but preparing them will require time and patience.

INGREDIENTS

4 medium tomatoes
125g (4½oz) mozzarella, grated
150g (5½oz) soft goat's cheese
4 tbsp pesto
4 tbsp olive oil
salt and freshly ground pepper
6 tbsp Vinaigrette (see page 45)
handful fresh basil leaves, to garnish

1 Cut the tomatoes in half and scoop the seeds into a bowl. Put the seeds in a sieve and strain; reserve the resulting juice. Place the tomatoes upside down on a plate for 5 minutes to drain. Add the juice that collects on the plate to the reserved juice.

2 In a bowl, mix together the cheeses, tomato juice, and pesto. Season, then fill each tomato half with the mixture. Brush the tomatoes with the olive oil and place them on a baking tray under a hot grill. Grill for about 5 minutes until golden.

3 Place the tomatoes on a large serving plate and drizzle with a little vinaigrette. Garnish each tomato with a basil leaf.

Preparation & cooking time
30 minutes

Serves 4

Nutritional notes
kcalories 446; protein 11g; carbohydrate 4g; total fat 43g, of which saturated fat 11g; fibre 1g; sodium 437mg

SAVOY CABBAGE WITH CELERIAC & CHESTNUTS

Chestnuts always remind me of Christmas and, with a rich, velvety Madeira sauce, this makes an ideal festive dish. The ramekins can be filled a few hours or a day in advance, then kept in the refrigerator and cooked just before serving.

INGREDIENTS

1 small savoy cabbage
75g (2¾oz) butter
½ celeriac, peeled and cut in 1cm (½ inch) dice
1 onion, finely chopped
1 garlic clove, crushed
100g (3½oz) button mushrooms, diced
125g (4½oz) can chestnuts, drained and chopped or 50g (1¾oz) dried chestnuts, reconstituted
6 tbsp double cream
1 small egg, beaten
3 tbsp vegetable suet, grated
salt and freshly ground pepper
freshly grated nutmeg

FOR THE TARRAGON SAUCE

25g (1oz) unsalted butter
75g (2¾oz) button mushrooms, thinly sliced
3 tomatoes, skinned, deseeded, and chopped (see page 39)
1 tbsp chopped fresh tarragon
150ml (¼ pint) Madeira Sauce (see page 44)

1 Prepare the cabbage leaves (see step 1, below) and shred the remaining cabbage as finely as possible with a sharp knife.

2 Heat half the butter and fry the celeriac for 5–8 minutes over a medium heat until golden. Add 2 tablespoons of water, cover, and braise for 15 minutes until the celeriac is tender and the liquid has evaporated.

3 Sauté the onion, garlic, mushrooms, and chestnuts in the remaining butter over a medium heat for 5 minutes. Add the shredded cabbage and cream, and cook over a low heat for 10 minutes until the vegetables are tender and the sauce thickened.

4 Transfer to a bowl and, when cool, mix in the egg, suet, and celeriac. Season with salt, pepper, and nutmeg. Stuff the cabbage leaves (see steps 2–3, below). Place the ramekins in a roasting tin. Pour in boiling water to come one-third of the way up the sides of the ramekins. Bake for 40 minutes.

5 For the sauce, heat the butter and fry the mushrooms for 3 minutes over a medium heat. Add the tomatoes and tarragon, and cook for 1 minute. Stir in the Madeira sauce and cook for 5 minutes over a low heat. Turn out the parcels. Serve with the sauce.

Oven preheated to 200°C/400°F/Gas 6

Preparation & cooking time 1 hour 45 minutes, plus 1 hour for the Madeira Sauce

Serves 4

Nutritional notes kcalories 438; protein 5g; carbohydrate 16g; total fat 39g, of which saturated fat 23g; fibre 5g; sodium 254mg

STUFFING THE CABBAGE

1 Remove eight outer cabbage leaves. Cut out the centre rib of each one and discard. Blanch the leaves in boiling water for 2 minutes.

2 Line each of four 8cm (3¼ inch) ramekins with a cabbage leaf, leaving no gaps, so that the leaf hangs over the sides. Spoon in the filling.

3 Place another leaf over the filling, tuck in over the filling, and bring the overhanging bottom leaf over the top. Press down lightly to seal.

ORIENTAL STUFFED AUBERGINES

Aubergines stuffed with Mediterranean ingredients have become a popular vegetarian dish, but I find that Oriental flavours work equally well and make an interesting change. If you would like a spicier version, simply add more finely chopped chilli, and a little more ginger and coriander.

INGREDIENTS

4 medium aubergines

6 tbsp peanut oil

1 onion, chopped

2 garlic cloves, crushed

1 red chilli, finely chopped

2.5cm (1 inch) piece fresh root ginger, chopped

1 tbsp coriander seeds

150g (5½oz) fresh spinach

8 water chestnuts, peeled and sliced

150g (5½oz) can chopped tomatoes

2 tbsp chopped fresh coriander, plus fresh coriander leaves, to garnish

1 tsp black sesame seeds

FOR THE SAUCE

150ml (¼ pint) Vegetable Stock (see page 44)

2 tbsp tamari or light soy sauce

½ tsp caster sugar

1 tbsp dry sherry

2 tbsp lemon juice

2 tsp cornflour, mixed to a paste with 1 tbsp cold water

salt and freshly ground pepper

Oven preheated to
180°C/350°F/Gas 4

Preparation & cooking time
1 hour 45 minutes, plus 1 hour for the stock

Serves 4

Nutritional notes
kcalories 251; protein 5g; carbohydrate 16g; total fat 19g, of which saturated fat 4g; fibre 6g; sodium 712mg

1 Cut a lid from the top of each aubergine and reserve, then remove a thin slice from each base. Sit the aubergines on a greased baking sheet, brush them all over with 2 tablespoons of the oil, and bake for 30–35 minutes. When cool, scoop out the flesh, leaving a 1cm (½ inch) shell. Chop the flesh.

2 Heat the remaining oil in a pan and fry the onion, garlic, chilli, ginger, and coriander seeds over a low heat for 5–8 minutes until the onions are tender. Stir in the spinach and chestnuts, raise the heat a little, and cook for 2 minutes.

3 Add the tomatoes to the pan with the fresh coriander. Simmer for 15–20 minutes. Mix in the aubergine flesh and season.

4 Stuff the aubergine shells with the mixture, place them on the baking sheet, with the lids on the side, and bake for 15–20 minutes.

5 For the sauce, bring the stock, tamari, sugar, sherry, and lemon juice to the boil. Lower the heat to a simmer, add the cornflour paste, and stir until thickened. Surround the aubergines with the sauce and sprinkle with the sesame seeds. Garnish with coriander leaves.

STUFFED ROAST ONIONS

Onions are a basic ingredient in so many dishes, but they deserve to play a starring role, too. Roast onions taste sweet and tender, combining well with this mushroom and cheese filling. You could serve them with a Fresh Tomato Sauce (see page 45).

INGREDIENTS

4 large onions, unpeeled

4 tbsp peanut or vegetable oil

1 garlic clove, crushed

150g (5½oz) chestnut mushrooms, diced or 50g (1¼oz) selection dried, wild mushrooms, soaked for 30 minutes, drained

1 tbsp fresh thyme leaves

1 tbsp chopped fresh parsley

25g (1oz) Cheddar, grated

2 tbsp freshly grated Parmesan

50g (1¾oz) fresh white breadcrumbs

salt and freshly ground pepper

1 Cook the onions in boiling, salted water for 8–10 minutes. Cool under cold running water for a few seconds, then pat dry.

2 Carefully peel off the outer skins then, using a sharp knife, cut the top off each onion and reserve. Carefully scoop out the flesh, leaving two or three outer layers of onion.

3 Finely chop the onion flesh. Heat half the oil in a frying pan, and fry the chopped onion and garlic over a low heat for about 5 minutes until soft. Add the mushrooms and herbs and cook for a further 4–5 minutes.

4 Remove from the heat and leave to cool slightly. Mix in the Cheddar and season to taste. Fill the onion shells with the mixture. Mix together the Parmesan and breadcrumbs, and sprinkle over the top.

5 Pour the remaining oil on top, and bake the onions on a baking sheet, with the tops on the side, for 20–25 minutes. Serve hot, with or without the tops.

Oven preheated to 200°C/400°F/Gas 6

Preparation & cooking time 1–1¼ hours, plus 30 minutes soaking time

Serves 4

Nutritional notes kcalories 270; protein 8g; carbohydrate 26g; total fat 16g, of which saturated fat 5g; fibre 4g; sodium 269mg

ITALIAN BAKED MUSHROOMS

Because the stuffing needs no pre-cooking, this is very quick to prepare. The stuffing is lighter than the usual breadcrumb-based stuffings, so the mushrooms make an ideal starter.

INGREDIENTS

8 large open-cup mushrooms

½ small onion, chopped

75g (2¾oz) sun-dried tomatoes, chopped

100g (3½oz) spinach, cooked

75g (2¾oz) mozzarella, diced

2 garlic cloves, crushed

½ tbsp chopped fresh parsley

1 tbsp chopped fresh basil

6 tbsp extra virgin olive oil, plus extra, to grease

salt and freshly ground pepper

FOR THE DRESSING

1 red chilli, deseeded and finely diced

8 fresh basil leaves, roughly chopped

50g (1¾oz) pine kernels

125ml (4fl oz) olive oil

2 tbsp balsamic vinegar

100g (3½oz) sun-dried tomatoes, chopped

1 Remove the stems from the mushrooms. Set the mushroom cups aside until the filling is ready, and dice the stems roughly.

2 Place the diced mushroom stems in a bowl with the onion, tomatoes, spinach, mozzarella, garlic, parsley, basil, and olive oil. Toss together and season well.

3 Fill the mushroom cups with the mixture, then place on a lightly oiled baking sheet. Bake for about 10–15 minutes until the cups are tender and the cheese in the stuffing has melted.

4 For the dressing, blend all the ingredients together. Place two mushrooms on each plate and drizzle with the dressing.

Oven preheated to 160°C/325°F/Gas 3

Preparation & cooking time 30 minutes

Serves 4

Nutritional notes kcalories 803; protein 10g; carbohydrate 4g; total fat 83g, of which saturated fat 13g; fibre 1g; sodium 585mg

POTATO BRANDADE WITH TRUFFLE OIL

These are essentially jacket potatoes, but the most luxurious version imaginable. Floury baking potatoes are most suitable — this recipe will not work with waxy varieties. The truffle oil in the dressing is so pungent that just a small amount gives a remarkably heady scent and flavour.

INGREDIENTS

5 medium to large baking potatoes
2 garlic cloves, crushed
1 egg yolk
4 tbsp extra virgin olive oil
50g (1¼oz) Parmesan shavings
salt and freshly ground pepper
8 fresh chives, to garnish

FOR THE DRESSING

1 tbsp white truffle oil
3 tbsp olive oil
1 tbsp balsamic vinegar
4 sun-dried tomatoes, chopped

1 Bake the potatoes for about 1 hour until cooked through.

Halve the potatoes lengthways and scoop the flesh into a bowl, leaving a 1cm (½ inch) shell. Discard two of the shells. Mix the garlic into the flesh and leave to cool a little before beating in the egg yolk. Drizzle in the olive oil, beating continuously; season.

2 Spoon the flesh back into the eight half shells. Place on a baking sheet and return to the oven for 2–3 minutes, to heat through. Blend together all the dressing ingredients and season. Top the potatoes with shavings of Parmesan, drizzle the dressing around or over the potatoes, and garnish with chives.

Oven preheated to 200°C/400°F/Gas 6

Preparation & cooking time
1 hour 25 minutes

Serves 4

Nutritional notes
kcalories 556; protein 13g; carbohydrate 55g; total fat 33g, of which saturated fat 7g; fibre 4g; sodium 359mg

CARIBBEAN CHRISTOPHENES

Members of the squash family, christophenes have a bland taste that combines well with spicy flavourings. They are very popular in Caribbean cookery, so I have given a Caribbean accent to the stuffing in this recipe, using coconut, chilli, and curry powder.

INGREDIENTS

4 medium christophenes
2 tomatoes, skinned and deseeded (see page 39)
4 tbsp clarified butter or vegetable oil
1 onion, chopped
1 garlic clove, crushed
4 cardamom seeds
½ tsp curry powder
1 green chilli, deseeded and finely chopped
125g (4½oz) sweetcorn
2 tbsp chopped fresh coriander
1 tbsp desiccated coconut

1 Boil the christophenes whole for 35 minutes until tender. Halve lengthways and scoop out

the flesh, leaving a 1cm (½ inch) shell. Reserve the flesh. Chop the tomatoes finely.

2 Heat 2 tablespoons of the butter in a frying pan. Fry the onion, garlic, cardamom, and curry powder over a medium heat for 5 minutes until soft. Mash the christophene pulp and add to the pan with the remaining ingredients. Heat through for 5 minutes.

3 Spoon the mixture into the christophene shells and drizzle the remaining butter over the top. Grill under a medium grill or bake for 8–10 minutes until golden. Serve hot.

Oven preheated to 200°C/400°F/Gas 6

Preparation & cooking time
1 hour 10 minutes

Serves 4

Nutritional notes
kcalories 238; protein 5g; carbohydrate 31g; total fat 12g, of which saturated fat 7g; fibre 6g; sodium 100mg

RED PEPPERS WITH FENNEL & CORN

Whole red peppers make perfect containers for this rich, creamy filling. With their golden crust of Parmesan and cornmeal, they look quite stunning. I love the flavour of caraway seeds, which echoes the fennel, but they are not to everyone's taste, so omit them if you prefer.

INGREDIENTS

4 red peppers

2 tbsp olive oil, plus extra, to grease

salt and freshly ground pepper

FOR THE FILLING

2 small fennel, chopped

150ml (¼ pint) double cream

2 garlic cloves, crushed

1 tsp caraway seeds

100g (3½oz) sweetcorn kernels

1 tbsp pine kernels, toasted

55g (2oz) Parmesan, grated

2 tbsp cornmeal

1 Slice the tops off the peppers and set them aside. Deseed the peppers. Brush the insides with oil and season. Put the peppers upright on an oiled baking sheet, and bake, with the tops on the side, for 12–15 minutes until tender.

2 For the filling, blanch the fennel in boiling water for 2–3 minutes until tender. Drain. Heat the cream with the garlic, caraway, and fennel over a low heat. Cook gently for 15 minutes until the sauce is thick. Add the sweetcorn and pine kernels. Season.

3 Fill the peppers with the fennel mixture. Mix together the Parmesan and the cornmeal and sprinkle over the peppers. Return to the oven for 5 minutes until golden. Replace the tops and serve.

Oven preheated to
200°C/400°F/Gas 6

Preparation &
cooking time
50–55 minutes

Serves 4

Nutritional notes
kcalories 421; protein 11g;
carbohydrate 23g;
total fat 32g, of which
saturated fat 15g;
fibre 6g; sodium 281mg

GOLDEN PEPPERS WITH COURGETTE PEPERONATA

This is the sort of food we are all supposed to be eating more of: lots of fresh vegetables lightly cooked in a little olive oil. With the lively flavours of chilli, capers, and olives, this recipe makes a great starter or light lunch dish.

INGREDIENTS

4 yellow peppers

2 tbsp olive oil, plus extra, to grease

salt and freshly ground pepper

FOR THE PEPERONATA

4 tbsp olive oil

1 onion, chopped

2 garlic cloves, crushed

½ tsp dried chilli flakes

300g (10½oz) baby courgettes, sliced

4 small tomatoes, halved

1 tbsp chopped fresh oregano

2 tbsp red wine vinegar

1 tbsp capers, rinsed and drained

1 tbsp pitted black olives, chopped

1 Slice the tops off the peppers and reserve the tops. Deseed the peppers. Brush the insides with the oil and season. Put the peppers upright on an oiled baking sheet, and bake, with the tops on, for 12–15 minutes until the peppers are lightly charred and just tender.

2 For the peperonata, heat the olive oil in a large frying pan, add the onion, and fry over a low heat for 5 minutes until soft. Add the garlic and chilli flakes, and cook for a further 2 minutes.

3 Add the courgettes and sauté for 1 minute, still over a low heat. Add the tomatoes, season, and cook gently, covered, for 8–10 minutes, until the tomatoes have softened and a sauce begins to form around the courgettes.

4 Remove the lid of the pan and add half the oregano. Stir well, then pour in the vinegar and add the capers and olives. Adjust the seasoning, then fill the roasted peppers with the mixture. Return the peppers to the oven for a further 15 minutes, sprinkle with the reserved oregano, replace the tops, and serve.

Oven preheated to
200°C/400°F/Gas 6

Preparation &
cooking time
50–55 minutes

Serves 4

Nutritional notes
kcalories 234; protein 4g;
carbohydrate 15g;
total fat 18g, of which
saturated fat 3g;
fibre 5g; sodium 166mg

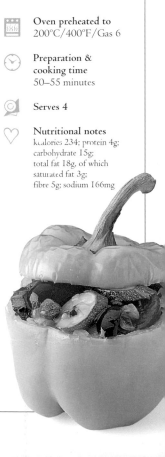

SALADS

THE FAMOUS 19TH-CENTURY gastronome Brillat Savarin once said of salad, "It freshens without enfeebling, and fortifies without irritating". Here is a selection of salads with a riot of tastes and textures, that are also deliciously fortifying. There are substantial salads combining cheese, noodles, or bread with crisp vegetables, and salads with Oriental, Middle Eastern, and Mediterranean influences. Some can be served as side dishes or starters, while others make spectacular main courses.

JAPANESE OMELETTE SALAD

KEY INGREDIENTS

Soy sauce is made from fermented soya beans and imparts sweetness and depth

Glutinous or sushi rice is a short- to medium-grain rice, prized for its sticky texture

Mangetouts are flat-podded peas that can be eaten whole

Yellow peppers add colour to salads and are packed with vitamins

Cucumber is always a welcome addition to salads with its cool, refreshing taste

Watercress has a wonderful peppery flavour and is rich in iron and calcium

Packed full of goodness, this salad has a perfect balance of tastes and textures. Strips of soft, lightly spiced, fluffy omelette make a delicious contrast to crisp, raw vegetables and sticky Japanese rice.

INGREDIENTS

FOR THE OMELETTE

4 eggs

1 tbsp soy sauce

2.5cm (1 inch) piece fresh root ginger, chopped

1 tbsp chopped fresh coriander

freshly ground pepper

40g (1½oz) butter

FOR THE SALAD

50g (1¼oz) glutinous or sushi rice, cooked

50g (1¼oz) mangetouts, trimmed and cut in strips

1 yellow pepper, deseeded and cut in julienne strips

4 spring onions, cut in strips

75g (2¾oz) cucumber, cut in thin strips

1 red pepper, deseeded and cut in julienne strips

100g (3½oz) watercress leaves

100ml (3½fl oz) Vinaigrette (see page 45)

1 For the salad, combine the rice, vegetables, watercress, and vinaigrette in a salad bowl, toss well, then set aside.

2 For the omelette, beat the eggs with the soy sauce, ginger, coriander, and pepper.

3 Melt half the butter in an omelette pan over a medium heat. When just bubbling, pour in half the egg mixture and swirl to coat the base of the pan. Fry for 5 minutes until golden and just set. Turn and cook the other side in the same way. Transfer to a plate and keep warm. Repeat the process to make a second omelette with the remaining mixture.

4 Arrange the salad on four plates. Slice the omelettes into thin strips, then arrange them on top of each serving of salad.

Preparation & cooking time
50 minutes

Serves 4

Nutritional notes
kcalories 370; protein 11g; carbohydrate 6g; total fat 34g, of which saturated fat 10g; fibre 2g; sodium 519mg

CAULIFLOWER SALAD WITH GRILLED PEPPERS

In this recipe sweet, roasted peppers and a punchy dressing made with capers, mustard, tarragon, and horseradish give simple cauliflower a real kick. It is important not to overcook the cauliflower florets, because they will soften further as they marinate.

INGREDIENTS

2 peppers (1 red, 1 green), roasted, peeled, and deseeded (see page 39)

1 large cauliflower

FOR THE DRESSING

100ml (3½fl oz) olive oil

2 tbsp tarragon vinegar

1 tbsp capers, drained and rinsed

1 garlic clove, crushed

1 tsp Dijon mustard

1 tbsp grated fresh horseradish

1 tomato, deseeded and finely diced

1 tbsp chopped fresh tarragon

salt and freshly ground pepper

1 Cut the peppers in strips and place on a warm plate. Set aside and keep warm.

2 Break the cauliflower into florets and cook them in a pan of boiling, salted water for 2 minutes until tender, but still firm to the bite.

3 Combine all the ingredients for the dressing in a bowl and add the peppers and cauliflower. Toss the vegetables well to coat them in the dressing and leave to marinate for 1 hour at room temperature before serving.

Preparation & cooking time
50 minutes, plus 1 hour marinating time

Serves 4

Nutritional notes
kcalories 299; protein 6g; carbohydrate 9g; total fat 27g, of which saturated fat 4g; fibre 4g; sodium 191mg

PEKING SEAWEED SALAD

Japanese or Chinese food stores are the places to visit to stock up on the ingredients for this salad. Pink ginger is a pickled ginger that is available in jars from Japanese food stores. Wakame seaweed is milder and softer than other seaweeds but, like all varieties, it is chock full of nutrients. Hijiki seaweed is a good alternative if wakame is not available.

INGREDIENTS

120g (4¼oz) wakame seaweed, soaked in water for 2 hours, then drained

¼ cucumber, halved, deseeded, and sliced

8 red radishes, thinly sliced

75g (2¾oz) mooli radish, thinly sliced

1 small courgette, thinly sliced

50g (1¾oz) peashoots, optional

20g (¾oz) pink ginger

200g (7oz) mixed salad leaves

black or toasted sesame seeds, to serve

salt and freshly ground pepper

FOR THE DRESSING

3 tbsp lime juice

1 tbsp chopped fresh mint

2 tbsp chopped fresh coriander

pinch dried chilli flakes

2 tbsp light soy sauce

2 tbsp granulated sugar

6 tbsp vegetable oil

2.5cm (1 inch) piece fresh root ginger, grated

1 For the dressing, blend together all the ingredients in a bowl, leave for 20 minutes to allow the flavours to infuse, then strain through a sieve into another bowl. Cover and set aside.

2 Place all the ingredients for the salad, except the mixed salad leaves, in a serving bowl. Mix well, then add the dressing. Cover and leave to marinate for 1 hour at room temperature.

3 Add the salad leaves to the salad and toss well. Sprinkle the sesame seeds on top, season to taste, and serve immediately.

Preparation & cooking time
40 minutes, plus 2 hours soaking time, plus 1 hour marinating time

Serves 4

Nutritional notes
kcalories 236; protein 7g; carbohydrate 8g; total fat 20g, of which saturated fat 2g; fibre 16g; sodium 1613mg

AVOCADO, PAPAYA & BRIE SALAD

This is a pretty and refreshing salad, topped with toasted cheese croutons. Other white-rinded, soft cheeses, apart from Brie, such as Bonchester or Camembert, would also be appropriate for this recipe.

INGREDIENTS

50g (1¾oz) French beans

200g (7oz) mixed salad leaves
(such as batavia, chicory, and young spinach)

1 avocado, cut in 1cm (½ inch) slices

1 papaya, cut in 1cm (½ inch) slices

125g (4½oz) ripe, but firm Brie, cut
in 5mm (¼ inch) slices

8 slices French bread, toasted

salt and freshly ground pepper

FOR THE DRESSING

4 tbsp olive oil

1 tbsp red wine vinegar

1 tsp Dijon mustard

1 tsp maple syrup

½ tbsp green peppercorns,
lightly crushed with a knife

1 Blanch the French beans in boiling, salted water for 4–5 minutes until tender, but still crisp. Drain the beans and refresh them in iced water, then pat them dry.

2 For the dressing, blend together all the ingredients in a bowl and season.

3 Place the salad leaves in a bowl with the French beans, avocado, and papaya, and add the dressing. Toss lightly to coat the leaves, then season. Divide the salad between four plates.

4 Place a slice of Brie on each of the toast slices. Place the toast slices on a baking sheet. Grill for about 4 minutes until the cheese melts.

5 To serve, place two warm, Brie-topped toasts on top of each salad and serve immediately.

⏱ **Preparation & cooking time**
25 minutes

◎ **Serves 4**

♡ **Nutritional notes**
kcalories 520; protein 15g;
carbohydrate 52g;
total fat 29g, of which
saturated fat 9g;
fibre 4g; sodium 838mg

ULTIMATE VEGETABLE SALAD

A garnish of toasted hazelnuts and a rich, creamy dressing lift this salad into a class of its own. The time to make it is early summer, when the vegetables are young and tender. Serve it as an elegant starter or light lunch.

INGREDIENTS

250g (9oz) French beans

2 carrots, cut in strips

50g (1¾oz) peas, cooked

1 celery stick, sliced

3 tomatoes, deseeded and chopped

100g (3½oz) little gem lettuce leaves

50g (1¾oz) hazelnuts, toasted

10 fresh basil leaves, shredded, to garnish

FOR THE DRESSING

150ml (¼ pint) crème fraîche

2 tbsp tomato purée

1 tbsp red wine vinegar

½ tsp Dijon mustard

½ garlic clove, crushed

salt and freshly ground pepper

1 Blanch the French beans in boiling, salted water for 4–5 minutes until tender, but still crisp. Drain and refresh in iced water, then pat dry. Blanch the carrots in boiling water for 30 seconds. Drain and refresh in iced water, then pat dry.

2 Mix together the beans, carrots, peas, celery, and tomatoes in a bowl.

3 For the dressing, mix together all the ingredients and season, then leave to infuse for 10 minutes. Pour the dressing over the vegetables, reserving a little for the lettuce leaves. Toss the salad well and season to taste.

4 Toss the lettuce leaves with the reserved dressing. Arrange them on a serving plate and lay the vegetables on top. Sprinkle with toasted hazelnuts and garnish with shredded basil leaves.

⏱ **Preparation & cooking time**
25 minutes

◎ **Serves 4**

♡ **Nutritional notes**
kcalories 214; protein 6g;
carbohydrate 12g;
total fat 16g, of which
saturated fat 5g;
fibre 5g; sodium 192mg

Artichoke, Rocket,
Pepper & Mushroom Salad

Artichoke, Rocket, Pepper & Mushroom Salad

Try to find only the smallest, most tender artichokes to use in this salad. If they are very small they will hardly need trimming at all. Slice them as thinly as possible for the tastiest results.

INGREDIENTS

4 small globe artichokes

juice of 2 lemons

4 tbsp olive oil

4 fresh lemon balm leaves or basil leaves

1 red pepper, roasted, peeled, deseeded
(see page 39), and cut in julienne strips

75g (2¼oz) button mushrooms,
thinly sliced

40g (1½oz) young rocket leaves

salt and cracked black pepper

1 Break the stalks off the artichokes. Remove the tough outer leaves, and trim the tops to about 2.5cm (1 inch) from the bases, so that just the tender leaves and the hearts are left.

2 Cut the artichokes in half lengthways, to expose the chokes (hairy inner fibres).

Remove the chokes with a spoon and squeeze lemon juice over the hearts to stop them going black.

3 Use a sharp knife to cut each artichoke half into very thin slices: take care as they are delicate.

4 Place the artichoke slices in a bowl with the oil and a little more lemon juice. Add the lemon balm leaves, roasted pepper, and mushrooms, and leave to marinate for 15–20 minutes.

5 Place the rocket leaves in a bowl, season lightly with salt, and dress with a little of the artichoke marinade. Gently mix together the artichoke slices, peppers, and mushrooms. Pile on to four serving plates. Scatter the cracked black pepper and the rocket leaves on top.

Preparation time
40 minutes, plus
15–20 minutes
marinating time

Serves 4

Nutritional notes
kcalories 152; protein 7g;
carbohydrate 8g;
total fat 12g, of which
saturated fat 2g;
fibre 1g; sodium 156mg

Potato Salad with Saffron Leeks & Mustard

Leeks and saffron are a perfect culinary combination. Here they make the base for an unusual, elegant potato salad. Jersey Royals are the best potatoes to use, but if these are unavailable, any good, waxy variety of salad potato will do.

INGREDIENTS

¼ tsp saffron strands,
or ½ tsp powdered saffron

100ml (3½fl oz) boiling water

salt

350g (12oz) baby leeks, trimmed

450g (1lb) Jersey Royal potatoes, scrubbed

½ tsp black mustard seeds

FOR THE DRESSING

1 tsp coarse-grain mustard

2 tbsp white wine vinegar

6 tbsp peanut or vegetable oil

2 tbsp snipped fresh chives

1 Place the saffron in a pan and cover with the boiling water. Add a little salt and bring to the boil. Reduce the heat and simmer for 1 minute, then add the leeks. Simmer the leeks for 2–3 minutes until tender. Drain and cool.

2 For the dressing, place the mustard and vinegar in a bowl with a little salt. Slowly add the oil, whisking all the time, to form an emulsion, then mix in the snipped chives.

3 Place the potatoes in a pan, cover with cold, salted water, bring to the boil, then reduce the heat. Simmer for 15–20 minutes. Drain, then allow to cool a little before slicing into rounds. Place the potatoes in a bowl and coat with the dressing, reserving a little for the leeks. Leave the potatoes to cool to room temperature.

4 Toss the leeks well in the reserved dressing and arrange on a serving plate. Pile the potatoes on top, sprinkle with black mustard seeds, and serve at room temperature.

**Preparation &
cooking time**
50 minutes

Serves 4

Nutritional notes
kcalories 252; protein 4g;
carbohydrate 21g;
total fat 18g, of which
saturated fat 4g;
fibre 3g; sodium 146mg

SINGAPORE NOODLE SALAD

Oriental noodles form the basis of some of the world's best fast-food dishes. Once the vegetables have been sliced, this tasty main course salad can be thrown together in no time at all.

INGREDIENTS

350g (12oz) egg noodles

150g (5½oz) sugar-snap peas

1 red pepper, halved, deseeded, and cut in julienne strips

2 carrots, cut in julienne strips

2 spring onions, shredded

100g (3½oz) shiitake mushrooms, sliced

25g (1oz) fresh coriander leaves

25g (1oz) cashew nuts, toasted

FOR THE DRESSING

4 tbsp peanut oil

1 garlic clove, crushed

1 green chilli, halved, deseeded, and chopped

3 tbsp rice wine vinegar

2.5cm (1 inch) piece fresh root ginger, grated

1 tbsp hoisin sauce

salt and freshly ground pepper

1 Cook the noodles according to packet instructions, drain, and refresh under cold, running water.

2 Blanch the sugar-snap peas in boiling, salted water for 1 minute. Drain and refresh them in iced water, then pat dry. Place all the vegetables except the mushrooms in a bowl. Set aside.

3 For the dressing, heat the oil in a pan, add the garlic and chilli, and stir-fry for 30 seconds. Throw in the mushrooms and sauté over a high heat for 2 minutes. Remove the mushrooms from the pan and add to the bowl with the vegetables. Add the remaining ingredients for the dressing to the pan and warm through.

4 Pour the dressing over the vegetables and toss. Make a mound of noodles on each serving plate and pile on the vegetables. Alternatively, mix together the dressing, vegetables, and noodles, and pile on to the plates. Top with coriander and cashew nuts.

Preparation & cooking time
30 minutes

Serves 4

Nutritional notes
kcalories 536; protein 15g; carbohydrate 75g; total fat 22g, of which saturated fat 5g; fibre 5g; sodium 485mg

CRAZY TOMATO SALAD

Make this in late summer when tomatoes are at their best. Full of concentrated tomato flavour, it combines two different types of fresh tomato with sweet, oven-dried tomatoes that have been infused with oil, basil, garlic, oregano, and coriander seeds.

INGREDIENTS

4–6 plum tomatoes

150ml (¼ pint) extra virgin olive oil

½ tsp coriander seeds

2 garlic cloves, peeled and thinly sliced

8 sprigs fresh basil

1 tbsp fresh oregano leaves

4–6 vine tomatoes, skinned (see page 39)

16 red cherry tomatoes

2 tbsp red wine vinegar

½ tbsp granulated sugar

150ml (¼ pint) tomato juice

2 tbsp dry vermouth

sea salt and cracked black pepper

1 Cut the plum tomatoes in half lengthways and lay them out on a baking sheet, with the cut sides facing upwards.

2 Season and drizzle with 2 tablespoons of oil. Place in the oven and leave to shrivel gently for 5–6 hours. When cooked, place the oven-dried tomatoes in a pan with the remaining oil, coriander seeds, garlic, basil, and oregano, and warm through on a very low heat for 15 minutes. Set aside.

3 Cut the vine and cherry tomatoes in half and add to the pan containing the oven-dried tomatoes. Transfer to a bowl. Combine the vinegar, sugar, tomato juice, and vermouth, and pour it over the tomatoes. Cover, and leave to marinate at room temperature for 6 hours. Sprinkle with salt and cracked black pepper and serve.

Oven preheated to 110°C/225°F/Gas ¼

Preparation & cooking time
5½–6½ hours, plus 6 hours marinating time

Serves 4

Nutritional notes
kcalories 407; protein 3g; carbohydrate 11g; total fat 39g, of which saturated fat 6g; fibre 3g; sodium 32mg

SALAD FIL FIL

This pleasant-tasting salad originated in North Africa. The name Fil Fil comes from a North African word for green peppers, which are used in this salad. Usually it does not include couscous, but I like to add this because it gives the salad additional texture. You can serve it with a fresh green salad, if you wish.

INGREDIENTS

100g (3½oz) couscous

4 large green peppers, roasted, peeled, deseeded (see page 39), and diced

4 ripe, but firm tomatoes, skinned, deseeded (see page 39), and diced

2 garlic cloves, crushed

1 fresh green chilli, deseeded and sliced

2 tbsp chopped fresh parsley

salt and freshly ground pepper

FOR THE DRESSING

6 tbsp olive oil

4 tbsp fresh lemon juice

1 tsp cumin seeds

1 Cook the couscous according to packet instructions. When cooked, place in a large bowl and mix in the peppers. Season well.

2 For the dressing, place the olive oil, lemon juice, cumin seeds, and seasoning in a bowl and whisk until well combined.

3 Mix the tomatoes and dressing into the couscous and peppers along with the remaining ingredients. Toss the salad, then check the seasoning.

4 Cover and leave to chill in the refrigerator for up to 2 hours to allow the flavours to develop. Serve lightly chilled.

Preparation & cooking time
50 minutes, plus 2 hours chilling time

Serves 4

Nutritional notes
kcalories 253; protein 4g; carbohydrate 21g; total fat 18g, of which saturated fat 3g; fibre 4g; sodium 116mg

MIDDLE EASTERN FLATBREAD & SUMAK SALAD

A salad for the thrifty – this is a great way of using up stale pitta bread. Sumak is a spice powder with an astringent, lemony flavour. You should be able to find it in Middle Eastern or Turkish delicatessens.

INGREDIENTS

1 cucumber, chopped

4 tomatoes, chopped

8 spring onions, chopped

1 green pepper, halved, deseeded, and chopped

100g (3½ oz) haricot beans, soaked overnight and cooked (see page 41)

12 pitted black olives

½ tbsp sumak

2 pitta breads, broken in small pieces

salt and freshly ground pepper

FOR THE DRESSING

1 tbsp fresh coriander, finely chopped

½ tbsp mint, finely chopped

1 garlic clove, crushed

8 tbsp olive oil

juice of 2 lemons

1 For the dressing, blend together all the ingredients in a mixing bowl until thoroughly combined.

2 Place all the vegetables in a bowl with the haricot beans, olives, half the sumak, and the dressing. Toss the vegetables to coat them with the dressing. Cover and leave to chill in the refrigerator before serving.

3 In a dry frying pan, toast the pitta bread pieces, shaking the pan from time to time until they are browned and crisp. Stir into the vegetables and season to taste. Transfer the salad to a serving bowl. Sprinkle the remaining sumak on top and serve.

Preparation & cooking time
1½–2 hours, plus overnight soaking time

Serves 4

Nutritional notes
kcalories 414; protein 11g; carbohydrate 40g; total fat 24g, of which saturated fat 4g; fibre 8g; sodium 521mg

PURPLE POTATO, ARTICHOKE & MILLET SALAD

Purple potatoes are the latest designer potatoes. They are a pretty colour and make a great addition to my new-look Niçoise salad. It has wonderful red, green, and white colours, as well as my favourite grain, millet.

INGREDIENTS

120g (4¼oz) millet
300g (10½oz) purple potatoes
120g (4¼oz) Jerusalem artichokes
50g (1¾oz) French beans, cooked
100g (3½oz) mixed yellow and red cherry tomatoes
3 hard-boiled eggs, quartered
20g (¾oz) pitted black olives, halved
2 garlic cloves, crushed
1 tbsp superfine capers, drained
2 shallots, finely chopped

FOR THE DRESSING

4 tbsp white wine vinegar
125ml (4fl oz) olive oil
50g (1¾oz) pine kernels, toasted
2 tbsp chopped fresh oregano
2 tbsp chopped fresh chives

1 For the dressing, blend together all the ingredients in a bowl, cover, and set aside.

2 Place the millet in a separate bowl, cover with boiling water, cover the bowl, and leave to stand for 10–15 minutes. Drain the millet and pat it dry with a cloth.

3 Cook the potatoes whole, in their skins, in a pan of boiling water for 15–20 minutes. Drain. When cool enough, peel and cut in 5mm (¼ inch) slices. Meanwhile, cook the artichokes in boiling water for 15 minutes, peel, and cut in 5mm (¼ inch) slices.

4 Combine all the ingredients in a bowl, add the dressing, mix well, and serve.

Preparation & cooking time
45 minutes

Serves 4

Nutritional notes
kcalories 627; protein 11g;
carbohydrate 43g;
total fat 45g, of which
saturated fat 6g;
fibre 3g; sodium 200mg

GOAT'S CHEESE & ROASTED SHALLOT SALAD

In this recipe the shallots are roasted with balsamic vinegar for an intensely sweet-sour flavour. They are the perfect partner for the goat's cheese, but they are equally good served as an accompaniment to other dishes.

INGREDIENTS

2 Capricorn goat's cheeses, halved crossways

250g (9oz) small shallots, peeled

100ml (3½fl oz) balsamic vinegar

1 tbsp granulated sugar

200g (7oz) small beetroots, cooked and cut in wedges

FOR THE MARINADE

150ml (¼ pint) olive oil

2 garlic cloves, sliced

1 tbsp chopped fresh thyme

2 tbsp chopped fresh rosemary

½ tsp black peppercorns, crushed

FOR THE DRESSING

100ml (3½fl oz) orange juice

2 tbsp walnut oil

50g (1¾oz) dried apricots, soaked in water for 2 hours and sliced

1 tbsp walnuts, roughly chopped

1 For the marinade, combine the ingredients in a bowl. Place the goat's cheeses in a shallow dish, and pour the marinade over. Cover and refrigerate overnight.

2 The following day, place the shallots in a roasting tin. Pour the marinade from the cheeses over the shallots; set aside the cheeses and cover. Add the balsamic vinegar, and sprinkle the sugar over the top. Bake for 45–50 minutes until the shallots are tender. Strain the juices left in the tin and reserve. Add the beetroot to the shallots and return to the oven to keep warm.

3 Blend together the dressing ingredients in a small bowl and add the strained juices from the shallots.

4 Place the cheeses on a baking sheet under a hot grill to warm through and soften slightly, but do not let them melt.

5 Place one portion of cheese on each plate and surround with the beetroot and shallots. Pour the dressing around the cheese and vegetables. Serve at room temperature.

Oven preheated to 200°C/400°F/Gas 6

Preparation & cooking time 1 hour 40 minutes, plus 2 hours soaking time, plus overnight marinating time

Serves 4

Nutritional notes kcalories 674; protein 10g; carbohydrate 22g; total fat 61g, of which saturated fat 12g; fibre 3g; sodium 300mg

GREEN LEAF SALAD WITH GARDEN HERBS

A good green salad must be made with care. Select only the freshest leaves, rinse and dry them thoroughly, and toss them with the dressing just before serving. The choice of herbs is up to you, but the more delicate varieties, such as chervil and basil, work best in this recipe.

INGREDIENTS

1 small garlic clove, halved

250g (9oz) mixed green salad leaves (such as lamb's lettuce, little gem, rocket, young sorrel leaves, frisée, and cos)

bunch mixed fresh herbs (such as basil, tarragon, chervil, flatleaf parsley, and mint)

4 slices French bread, toasted

1 tbsp Dijon mustard

FOR THE DRESSING

1 shallot, finely chopped

½ tsp herb mustard

2 tbsp Champagne vinegar

125ml (4fl oz) extra virgin olive oil

salt

1 Rub the inside of a large bowl liberally with the cut side of the garlic clove. Toss the leaves and herbs in the bowl.

2 For the dressing, mix together the shallot, herb mustard, Champagne vinegar, and a little salt. Slowly whisk in all but 1 tablespoon of the oil until an emulsion is formed. Drizzle the dressing over the leaves and herbs and toss well.

3 Brush the toasted bread slices on both sides with the remaining oil and spread with Dijon mustard. Arrange the toasted bread on top of the salad.

Preparation & cooking time 20 minutes

Serves 4

Nutritional notes kcalories 404; protein 5g; carbohydrate 24g; total fat 33g, of which saturated fat 5g; fibre 1g; sodium 261mg

DESSERTS

CHOOSE A DESSERT to complement your main course, or build the rest of your meal around a spectacular finale. Here are recipes for every occasion: refreshing fresh fruit poached in an aromatic spiced syrup; delicate ice creams; nursery puddings such as treacle tart; and for chocolate lovers – a rich chocolate tart with chilli oil. Desserts are not immune to global influences, and I have included sweet things from the Middle East, Mexico, and the Mediterranean.

SAFFRON PEACHES WITH SUMMER BERRIES

KEY INGREDIENTS

Star anise has an aniseed flavour and interesting shape

Lemon counterbalances the sweetness of desserts with a pleasant tang

Summer berries give a splash of colour and sweetness to many desserts

Peaches are sweet and juicy whether eaten raw or lightly poached

Cinnamon imparts warmth and sweetness to sweet and savoury dishes

Saffron has a rich, yellow colour and a pungent, sweet scent

*T*ry to get white peaches for this delicate and refreshing summer dessert; sweeter than yellow ones, their pale flesh makes a pleasing contrast to the scarlet berries.

INGREDIENTS

4 ripe peaches (white if possible)

½ bottle dry white wine or champagne

250g (9oz) caster sugar

4 star anise

1 vanilla pod (or 1 tsp vanilla extract)

2 cinnamon sticks

½ lemon, cut in 3mm (⅛ inch) slices

¼ tsp fresh saffron strands

220g (7¼oz) mixed summer berries

1 Bring a large pan of water to the boil, add the peaches, and poach for 1–2 minutes. Remove the peaches from the pan and, when cool, peel them carefully.

2 In a separate large pan, combine the wine with 300ml (½ pint) water, the sugar, star anise, vanilla pod, cinnamon, lemon, and saffron strands.

3 Boil the liquid until it becomes syrupy, then lower the heat, and add the peaches. If there is not enough liquid to cover the peaches, add more water. Cover with a piece of greaseproof paper, and simmer for 15–20 minutes. Remove the peaches and set aside.

4 Raise the heat and boil the syrup until it is reduced by one-third. Remove from the heat and leave to cool for a few minutes before returning the peaches to the pan. Leave to cool.

5 Transfer the peaches to a serving bowl and scatter the berries on top. Strain the syrup into a jug, reserve the cinnamon and star anise, then pour the syrup over the peaches. Cover and chill for 4 hours. Decorate with the cinnamon and star anise.

Preparation & cooking time
1 hour, plus 4 hours chilling time

Serves 4

Nutritional notes
kcalories 349; protein 1g; carbohydrate 78g; total fat 0.2g, of which saturated fat 0.03g; fibre 2g; sodium 11mg

HAZELNUT TORTE WITH KIRSCH & BLUEBERRIES

Although this looks complicated to make, it is actually quite simple — a straightforward hazelnut meringue filled with flavoured cream and blueberries. Meringue circles can be made up to 24 hours in advance, then kept in an airtight container until ready for use.

INGREDIENTS

FOR THE TORTE
2 egg whites

125g (4½oz) caster sugar

¼ tsp baking powder

125g (4½oz) hazelnuts, coarsely ground

FOR THE KIRSCH CREAM
150ml (¼ pint) whipping or double cream

75g (2¾oz) icing sugar

zest and juice of ½ lemon

6 tbsp kirsch

FOR THE BLUEBERRY SAUCE
250g (9oz) fresh blueberries

55g (2oz) icing sugar, plus extra, to dust

juice of 1 lemon

blackberry leaves or mint leaves, to decorate

1 For the torte, whisk the egg whites and sugar until standing in stiff peaks. Whisk in the baking powder, then fold in the hazelnuts.

2 Pipe eight circles of the mixture, each measuring about 7.5cm (3 inches), on to silicone paper. Bake for about 30 minutes, until you can lift the circles cleanly off the paper. Cool.

3 For the cream, whisk together the cream and icing sugar until lightly whipped. Add the lemon zest and juice, and the kirsch, and continue to whisk until stiff.

4 For the sauce, in a blender or food processor blend 150g (5½oz) of the blueberries with the icing sugar and lemon juice until smooth, then strain through a fine sieve.

5 To serve, pipe the cream on to four meringues, pour over the sauce, and top with the remaining meringues. Decorate with the remaining berries and blackberry leaves, and dust with icing sugar.

Oven preheated to 160°C/325°F/Gas 3

Preparation & cooking time 50 minutes

Serves 4

Nutritional notes kcalories 550; protein 3g; carbohydrate 82g; total fat 22g, of which saturated fat 12g; fibre 2g; sodium 81mg

BAKED FIGS WITH DRIED FRUIT & ANISETTE

Dark purple figs have a wonderful flavour and are the best figs for this dish. I like to serve the figs hot, as a contrast to the chilled, vanilla-flavoured cream, but they are also very good served cold.

INGREDIENTS
100g (3½oz) selection of dried fruit, such as apricots, prunes, dates, and sultanas

8 large, ripe, fresh figs

2 tbsp honey or caster sugar

zest and juice of 1 orange

¼ tsp ground cardamom seeds

pinch fennel seeds

6 tbsp anisette liqueur, such as Pernod, or brandy (optional)

1 tbsp pine nuts, toasted

fresh mint sprigs, to decorate

TO SERVE
few drops vanilla extract

100ml (3½fl oz) crème fraîche or mascarpone

1 In a large bowl, soak the dried fruit in water overnight. Drain, then cut into small pieces.

2 Cut the fresh figs in half, scoop out the centres, then fill each fig half with the dried fruit.

3 Place the figs in a baking dish. Combine the honey, orange zest and juice, cardamom, fennel seeds, and anisette liqueur, if using, and pour over the figs. Cover, then bake for 20 minutes, basting with the juices occasionally.

4 Place the figs on a serving plate, pour the juice over them, and sprinkle the pine nuts on top. Decorate with fresh mint. Stir the vanilla extract into the crème fraîche until well combined and serve with the figs.

Oven preheated to 160°C/325°F/Gas 3

Preparation & cooking time 35 minutes, plus overnight soaking time

Serves 4

Nutritional notes kcalories 349; protein 4g; carbohydrate 44g; total fat 15g, of which saturated fat 8g; fibre 3g; sodium 35mg

PROSECCO-MASCARPONE & RASPBERRY SYLLABUB

For this luscious dessert, raspberries are marinated in Italian sparkling wine, then topped with a rich, creamy, orange-scented syllabub, and decorated with a sprinkling of white chocolate shavings and crushed Amaretti biscuits. This is easy to make, and devastatingly good.

INGREDIENTS

350g (12oz) raspberries

6 tbsp Prosecco
(or other sparkling white wine)

250g (9oz) mascarpone

zest and juice of 1 orange

25g (1oz) icing sugar,
or 1 tbsp honey

4 tbsp sweet white wine

TO DECORATE

50g (1¾oz) white chocolate shavings

6 Amaretti biscuits, crushed

1 Place the raspberries in a bowl, pour the Prosecco over the top, then cover with clingfilm and leave to marinate overnight, or for at least 2 hours.

2 Remove one-third of the raspberries, and push them through a fine sieve to remove any pips. Add the resulting raspberry purée to the remaining raspberries and mix together gently, then set aside.

3 In a bowl, lightly whisk together the mascarpone, the orange zest and juice, icing sugar, and sweet white wine. Divide the fruit between four tall, thin glasses. Spoon the mascarpone mixture on top of the fruit.

4 Leave to chill in the refrigerator for about 4 hours. Decorate with the white chocolate shavings and the crushed Amaretti biscuits before serving.

Preparation time
½ hour, plus
at least 2 hours
marinating time
(preferably overnight),
plus 4 hours
chilling time

Serves 4

Nutritional notes
kcalories 330; protein 12g;
carbohydrate 45g;
total fat 10g, of which
saturated fat 3g;
fibre 25g; sodium 44mg

PINK GRAPEFRUIT & ROSEWATER GRANITA

This pretty pink granita has an intriguing, exotic taste due to the inclusion of rosewater, which was a popular flavouring in Elizabethan Britain. Rosewater is also associated with Middle Eastern cookery, where it is used in both sweet and savoury dishes.

INGREDIENTS

25ml (1fl oz) rosewater

100g (3½oz) caster sugar

freshly grated zest of 1 pink grapefruit

300ml (½ pint) freshly squeezed
pink grapefruit juice

TO SERVE

pink grapefruit segments (all pith removed)

fresh raspberries

1 Place the rosewater and sugar in a pan with 425ml (¾ pint) water, and bring to the boil. When the liquid has reduced by almost half its original volume, remove from the heat, and add the grapefruit zest and juice.

2 Pour into a shallow pan or baking dish, and place in the freezer. Every half an hour, stir up the mixture roughly with a fork, to give an icy, crystalline texture.

3 Leave to freeze for up to 6 hours before serving. To serve, place two scoops of granita in each bowl, and surround with segments of fresh pink grapefruit and fresh raspberries.

Preparation time
30 minutes,
plus 6 hours
freezing time

Serves 8

Nutritional notes
kcalories 124; protein 1g;
carbohydrate 31g;
total fat 0.3g, of which
saturated fat 0.01g;
fibre 0.7g; sodium 5mg

APPLE & RHUBARB PIZZA

Pizzas have been topped with just about everything from smoked salmon to eggs and bacon, but have you ever tried a sweet pizza? In this recipe, the pizza is topped with a ginger-spiced rhubarb purée and thin slices of caramelized apple. Serve with Rhubarb Sorbet (see below).

INGREDIENTS

FOR THE PIZZA BASE

15g (½oz) fresh yeast

150ml (¼ pint) tepid water

225g (8oz) plain flour

4 tbsp caster sugar, plus extra, to sprinkle

FOR THE RHUBARB TOPPING

300g (10½oz) rhubarb, cubed

50g (1¾oz) caster sugar

15g (½oz) stem ginger, finely chopped

FOR THE APPLE TOPPING

4 apples, peeled, cored, and thinly sliced

50g (1¾oz) unsalted butter, melted

Rhubarb Sorbet (see below), to serve

1 For the pizza base, dissolve the yeast in the water and, when frothy, pour on to the flour and sugar in a bowl. Stir to combine, then knead to form a smooth dough. Cover the bowl with a damp cloth and leave for 20–30 minutes in a warm place until doubled in size.

2 Meanwhile, place the rhubarb in a medium pan with the sugar and ginger. Bring to the boil, lower the heat, and simmer for 20–25 minutes until nearly all the liquid has evaporated and the rhubarb is syrupy. Leave to cool.

3 When the dough has risen, knock it back by pushing it with your fists. Roll out the dough into one large rectangle. Place on a sheet of silicone paper on a baking tray.

4 Spread the rhubarb evenly over the base, then lay the apple slices, overlapping, over the top. Brush the pizza with melted butter and leave in a warm place to prove for a further 30 minutes. Sprinkle with a little caster sugar and bake for 20–25 minutes until the apples are golden and the pizza is crispy. Serve with rhubarb sorbet (see below).

Oven preheated to 200°C/400°F/Gas 6

Preparation & cooking time
1–1¼ hours, plus 1 hour proving time

Serves 6

Nutritional notes
kcalories 319; protein 5g; carbohydrate 61g; total fat 8g, of which saturated fat 5g; fibre 3g; sodium 7mg

RHUBARB SORBET

Rhubarb has a slight image problem, perhaps because many of us were forced to eat stewed rhubarb when we were children. Young, pink rhubarb has a much better flavour than the coarse old stems, and makes a very refreshing sorbet. This sorbet is particularly good served with the Apple & Rhubarb Pizza (see above).

INGREDIENTS

250g (9oz) caster sugar

250g (9oz) rhubarb, chopped

juice of 1 lemon

1 Place all the ingredients in a heavy-bottomed pan with 500ml (18fl oz) water and bring to the boil. Lower the heat, then simmer for about 10 minutes until the rhubarb is well cooked and the liquid is syrupy.

2 Transfer the mixture to a blender or food processor and blend until smooth. Put the mixture in a bowl and leave until thoroughly cooled.

3 Pour the mixture into an ice-cream maker and freeze-churn according to the manufacturer's instructions. If you do not have an ice-cream maker, place the mixture in a plastic box. Cover the box and freeze for 3–4 hours until half frozen. Whisk the mixture with an electric hand whisk; freeze for a further 3 hours. Whisk again, then freeze for 4–6 hours before serving.

Preparation time
35 minutes, plus 10–13 hours freezing time

Serves 8

Nutritional notes
kcalories 125; protein 0.3g; carbohydrate 33g; total fat 0.03g, of which saturated fat 0g; fibre 0.4g; sodium 3mg

CHOCOLATE & CHILLI OIL TART

This is not so strange as it sounds. Mexican cooks often include a little chocolate in spicy dishes, so I decided to turn the tables and add chilli oil to chocolate. It gives a warmth and depth of flavour that counterbalances the sweetness beautifully. This is one of my favourite desserts.

INGREDIENTS

FOR THE WALNUT PASTRY

250g (9oz) plain flour, plus extra, to dust

50g (1¾oz) ground walnuts

75g (2¾oz) caster sugar

150g (5½oz) softened unsalted butter, plus extra, to grease

1 egg, beaten

FOR THE FILLING

2 eggs, beaten

6 egg yolks, beaten

70g (2½oz) caster sugar

370g (13oz) dark chocolate couverture

1 tsp chilli oil

250g (9oz) unsalted butter

icing sugar, to dust

1 For the pastry, sift the flour into a bowl, add the walnuts, sugar, and butter, and stir until the mixture forms a crumble. Add the egg, stir to bind the ingredients together, and gently knead to a smooth pastry. Cover and chill in the refrigerator for at least 4 hours.

2 Grease a 20–23cm (8–9 inch) diameter flan case. Roll out the pastry to line the flan case; allow a 1cm (½ inch) overlap. Cover with greaseproof paper, fill with baking beans, and place on a baking sheet.

3 Bake blind for 10 minutes. Remove the baking beans and paper, and bake for 10 minutes more. If there are any cracks in the pastry, seal with beaten egg and bake for 2 minutes more. Cool.

4 For the filling, beat together the eggs, egg yolks, and sugar in a bowl. Melt the chocolate in a bowl over a pan of simmering water (ensuring that the water does not touch the bowl). When it has melted, add the oil and butter and mix well. Stir into the eggs.

5 Pour the chocolate mixture into the tart shell and bake for 10 minutes until set. Remove from the tin. Dust with icing sugar and serve at room temperature.

Oven preheated to 200°C/400°F/Gas 6

Preparation & cooking time 1–1¼ hours, plus 4 hours resting time

Serves 8

Nutritional notes kcalories 915; protein 12g; carbohydrate 74g; total fat 66g, of which saturated fat 37g; fibre 2g; sodium 49mg

BUTTERNUT SOUFFLE WITH BLACKBERRIES

This is a new twist on an old favourite. Here I use shallow pans or tins as the cooking vessels, rather than the more usual soufflé dish. I think that this adds a little more elegance to the soufflé and, nestled on a tart blackberry sauce, it is a flavour sensation.

Oven preheated to 190°C/375°F/Gas 5

Preparation & cooking time 1 hour 20 minutes

Serves 8

Nutritional notes
kcalories 251; protein 8g; carbohydrate 32g; total fat 10g, of which saturated fat 5g; fibre 2g; sodium 86mg

INGREDIENTS

175g (6oz) peeled butternut squash, chopped

40g (1½oz) unsalted butter, plus extra, to grease

40g (1½oz) strong plain flour

zest of 1 orange

3 tbsp Grand Marnier (or other orange liqueur)

400ml (14fl oz) hot milk

5 eggs, separated

85g (3oz) caster sugar

15g (½oz) cornflour

FOR THE BLACKBERRY SAUCE

300g (10½oz) blackberries

50g (1¼oz) icing sugar, plus extra, to dust

juice of ½ lemon

julienne of orange zest, to decorate

1 Place the squash in a pan with 250ml (9fl oz) water, bring to the boil, then simmer for 15 minutes until soft. Drain, then blend or finely mash the squash until smooth. Leave to cool.

2 Melt the butter in a pan over a medium heat, then beat in the flour, using a wooden spoon, until the mixture leaves the sides of the pan. Add the squash purée, orange zest, and Grand Marnier, and beat thoroughly until well combined.

3 Gradually pour the hot milk into the pan, beating all the time, and cook over a gentle heat for 5 minutes, stirring often. Pour into a large bowl, then leave to cool slightly before beating in the egg yolks, one at a time. Set aside.

4 Whisk together the egg whites, sugar, and cornflour until standing in stiff peaks. Beat one-third of the whites into the squash mixture, then gently fold in the remaining two-thirds with a metal spoon until well combined.

5 Grease eight blini pans or eight individual non-stick tart tins, 7cm (2¾ inches) in diameter. Dust the bases and sides with caster sugar, then fill two-thirds full with the soufflé mix. Place the blini pans in the oven or, if using the tartlet tins, place in a shallow baking tin and pour in hot water to come one-third of the way up the sides of the tins. Bake for 15–20 minutes until the soufflés are risen and golden.

6 For the sauce, blend together 200g (7oz) blackberries, the icing sugar, and lemon juice in a blender or food processor, then strain through a fine sieve.

7 Pour a little sauce on to each plate, top with the remaining whole blackberries, then place the soufflés on top, straight from the oven. Scatter the julienne of orange zest around the outside, dust with icing sugar, and serve.

ALMOND & HONEY FUDGE TART

Rich and moreish, the almond-studded fudge filling makes this a dessert to savour. This truly is a pièce de résistance.

INGREDIENTS
FOR THE PASTRY
350g (12oz) plain flour, plus extra, to dust

pinch of salt

2 tbsp icing sugar

250g (9oz) cold, unsalted butter, cut in pieces, plus extra, to grease

FOR THE FILLING
275g (9½oz) caster sugar

225g (8oz) blanched whole almonds

100g (3½oz) unsalted butter

150ml (¼ pint) milk

2 tbsp acacia honey

1 For the pastry, sift the flour, salt, and sugar into a large bowl. Cut the butter into the flour with a knife, then rub it into the mixture until it resembles fine breadcrumbs. Sprinkle in enough cold water to bind the mixture. Gather the pastry into a ball. Cover and leave to rest in the refrigerator for 1 hour.

2 Meanwhile, for the filling, bring the sugar and 150ml (¼ pint) water to the boil, and stir until the sugar has dissolved. Boil rapidly for about 5 minutes until the mixture begins to caramelize.

3 When pale brown, remove from the heat. Stir in the almonds and butter, then stir in the milk. Return to a low heat, and simmer for 15–20 minutes until the mixture becomes quite thick. Remove from the heat, and stir in the honey. Leave to cool slightly.

4 Meanwhile, lightly grease a 20–23cm (8–9 inch) flan tin. Roll out two-thirds of the dough and use to line the tin. Prick the bottom. Pour in the filling. Cover with the remaining dough, dampen the edges with water and press to seal them. Make a small vent in the centre. Bake for 40 minutes until golden. Cool before serving.

Oven preheated to 200°C/400°F/Gas 6

Preparation & cooking time 1½ hours, plus 1 hour resting time

Serves 10

Nutritional notes kcalories 668; protein 9g; carbohydrate 67g; total fat 43g, of which saturated fat 20g; fibre 3g; sodium 97mg

CHILLED MELON & SAGO SOUP

This is an Asian-inspired soup, served in individual melons. It is important to achieve the right balance of sweet and sour, so keep tasting as you add the lime juice and maple syrup. If you wish, you can scoop out the melon flesh and blend it together with the milk in a blender or food processor, but I prefer to eat the soup first and the melon later

INGREDIENTS
4 small charentais or galia melons

wedge of watermelon, cut in 1cm (½ inch) cubes

wedge of honeydew melon, cut in 1cm (½ inch) cubes

FOR THE SOUP
200g (7oz) sago

300ml (½ pint) milk

150ml (¼ pint) coconut milk

50ml (2fl oz) double cream

juice of 1 lime

maple syrup, to taste

1 Cut a thin slice off the base of each whole melon so that it sits upright. Slice the top off each one about 4cm (1½ inches) down. Remove the seeds from inside each

melon with a large metal spoon. Refrigerate the melon shells while you prepare the soup.

2 For the soup, place the sago in a pan, cover with water, and bring to the boil. Reduce the heat and simmer for 40–45 minutes, stirring regularly. When cooked, refresh under cold running water. Drain well and leave to go cold.

3 In a bowl, mix together the milk, coconut milk, and cream, then add the lime juice and maple syrup to sweeten to your taste. Finally, add the sago and mix together. Chill the soup for up to 4 hours in the refrigerator. Divide the cubes of melon between the melon shells, then divide the soup between the shells. Serve chilled.

Preparation time 1 hour, plus 4 hours chilling time

Serves 4

Nutritional notes kcalories 363; protein 3g; carbohydrate 73g; total fat 8g, of which saturated fat 5g; fibre 0.9g; sodium 124mg

OATMEAL TREACLE TART

For me, the secret of a good treacle tart is to include lots of lemon juice to offset the sweetness. In this version, oats are added to the filling instead of the more usual breadcrumbs, giving a delicious, wholesome mixture, rather like flapjacks.

INGREDIENTS

butter, to grease

300g (10½oz) Sweet Pastry (see page 42)

300ml (½ pint) golden syrup

75g (2¾oz) porridge oats

zest and juice of 1 large lemon

pinch of ground ginger

1 Grease a 20cm (8 inch) tart tin. On a floured surface, roll out the pastry and use to line the tin.

2 Warm the golden syrup gently in a medium pan over a low heat. Stir in the porridge oats, then the lemon zest and juice, and the ginger. Heat gently until the mixture is slightly runny in texture.

3 Pour the mixture into the prepared pastry case and bake for about 25 minutes. Leave to cool for 10–15 minutes: the filling will firm up as it cools. Serve the tart warm.

Oven preheated to 200°C/400°F/Gas 6

Preparation & cooking time
1 hour, plus 40 minutes for the pastry

Serves 4

Nutritional notes
kcalories 546; protein 6g; carbohydrate 100g; total fat 17g, of which saturated fat 9g; fibre 2g; sodium 219mg

FROZEN LEMON YOGURT & PEPPER CHERRIES

This tangy yogurt dessert goes back a long way in my repertoire, although the pepper cherries are a new addition. The peppercorns add an extra bite to the sweet cherry compote.

INGREDIENTS

2 eggs

50g (1¾oz) caster sugar

zest and juice of 3 lemons

125g (4½oz) Greek yogurt

75ml (2½fl oz) double cream, lightly whipped

FOR THE CHERRY COMPOTE

75g (2¾oz) caster sugar

25g (1oz) unsalted butter

½ tbsp lemon juice

1 tsp green peppercorns

450g (1lb) fresh cherries

maraschino liqueur or kirsch, to taste (optional)

mint leaves, to decorate

1 Place the eggs, sugar, and lemon zest and juice in a bowl, and set over a pan of gently simmering water, making sure that the water is not touching the base of the bowl. Whisk until the mixture is pale and thick, and has doubled in volume.

2 Remove the bowl from the pan, and continue to whisk until the mixture cools. When cool, fold in the yogurt gently with a metal spoon, then lightly fold in the whipped cream.

3 Place four 5cm (2 inch) metal ring moulds, or individual ramekins, on a baking sheet. Fill with the yogurt cream and smooth the tops with a knife. Freeze for 3 hours before serving.

4 For the cherry compote, heat the sugar, butter, lemon juice, and peppercorns over a high heat until the sugar and butter lightly caramelize. Add the cherries and liqueur, if using, then put a flame to the sauce to flambé off the alcohol. Reduce the heat, add 4 tablespoons of water, and simmer the cherries until just soft.

5 Loosen the yogurts from the moulds with a thin-bladed knife. Turn out on to serving plates. Pour the cherry compote over the yogurts, and decorate with mint leaves.

Preparation time
30 minutes, plus 3 hours freezing time

Serves 4

Nutritional notes
kcalories 403; protein 7g; carbohydrate 50g; total fat 20g, of which saturated fat 11g; fibre 1g; sodium 100mg

WINTER TRIFLE

This unusual trifle is made with caramelized pears and a light sponge layer that has been flavoured with coffee and rum, just like an Italian tiramisù. You may be worried about using custard powder, but in fact I use it a lot in desserts; it is a good, convenient product and should not be ignored.

INGREDIENTS

100g (3½oz) caster sugar

4 large pears, peeled, cored, and cut horizontally in 5mm (¼ inch) thick slices

2 tbsp dark rum

2 tbsp Camp coffee

24 sponge fingers or 1 plain sponge, cut in 2cm (¾ inch) cubes

100ml (3½fl oz) double cream, semi-whipped

FOR THE CUSTARD

600ml (1 pint) milk

3 tbsp custard powder

1 tbsp caster sugar

TO DECORATE

toasted hazelnuts

mint leaves

1 In a heavy-bottomed pan, heat the sugar over a high heat until it caramelizes. Add the pears, and turn them until they are soft and golden, and are coated in the caramel. Remove the pears and put in a bowl. Stir 100ml (3½fl oz) water, the rum, and the coffee into the syrup, then pour the mixture over the sponge fingers in a bowl.

2 For the custard, mix a little milk with the custard powder. Stir to a paste. Bring the remaining milk and sugar nearly to the boil, then pour on to the paste, stirring. Return the custard to the pan, and bring to the boil, stirring. Lower the heat and cook for 1–2 minutes, still stirring. Pour into a bowl, cool, then cover with clingfilm.

3 Place a few sponge fingers in the base of each of four glasses, top with pear slices, then some custard; repeat these layers. Finish with a layer of whipped cream. Serve chilled, decorated with toasted hazelnuts and mint leaves.

Preparation & cooking time
40 minutes, plus 2 hours chilling time

Serves 4

Nutritional notes
kcalories 648; protein 10g; carbohydrate 103g; total fat 22g, of which saturated fat 11g; fibre 4g; sodium 210mg

ITALIAN CREME CARAMEL

This is a version of crème caramel that I borrowed from a friend of mine. The recipe has been in his family for years. The chocolate is delicate and subtle – an interesting variation on the original.

INGREDIENTS

FOR THE BASE CARAMEL

100g (3½oz) caster sugar

vegetable oil, for greasing

FOR THE CREME

500ml (18fl oz) milk

½ vanilla pod, split down the middle

35g (1¼oz) white chocolate

3 eggs

1 egg yolk

85g (3oz) caster sugar

TO SERVE

1 orange, segmented

2 punnets fresh raspberries

white chocolate leaves, or shavings

1 For the caramel, heat the sugar in a heavy-bottomed pan. When it starts to melt, begin to stir slowly, but continuously. When dissolved, add 3 tablespoons of water, and stir until syrupy. Pour 3mm (⅛ inch) caramel into each of six lightly greased dariole moulds.

2 For the crème, heat the milk with the vanilla pod and bring to the boil. Remove from the heat, add the chocolate, and allow it to melt off the heat.

3 In a bowl, whisk together the eggs, egg yolk, and sugar, then slowly pour on the chocolate milk, stirring. To prevent the eggs from curdling, ensure that the milk is not too hot. Remove the vanilla pod. Strain the mixture through a fine sieve.

4 Divide the crème between the moulds, then place in a deep baking dish. Pour in boiling water to come two-thirds of the way up the sides. Bake for 20–25 minutes.

5 Cool, then chill in the refrigerator for 2 hours. Turn out the crème caramels on to serving plates. Pour any caramel left in the moulds over the tops. Serve with orange segments, raspberries, and chocolate leaves.

Oven preheated to
150°C/300°F/Gas 2

Preparation & cooking time
50 minutes, plus 2 hours chilling time

Serves 6

Nutritional notes
kcalories 454; protein 9g; carbohydrate 84g; total fat 11g, of which saturated fat 5g; fibre 3g; sodium 108mg

CANDIED AUBERGINE & CARDAMOM ICE-CREAM

Aubergines may seem an unlikely ingredient for a dessert, but they are often candied or made into sweet preserves in the Middle East. Here, they are combined with another Eastern flavour, cardamom, to make a fragrant but fresh-tasting dessert. If you do not have an ice-cream maker, follow the recipe for Rhubarb Sorbet (see page 128).

INGREDIENTS

150g (5½oz) aubergine, cut in small cubes

250g (9oz) caster sugar

2 tbsp aniseed liqueur (optional)

500ml (18fl oz) milk

250ml (9fl oz) double cream

10 fresh cardamom pods, split

1 egg

4 egg yolks

1 Place the aubergine and 50g (1¾oz) sugar in a pan, and cook over a high heat for 5–8 minutes until the aubergine turns golden. Add 200ml (7fl oz) water and the liqueur, if using, and simmer for 10 minutes

until the aubergine is soft and the water absorbed. Set aside.

2 Bring the milk, cream, and cardamom to the boil; set aside. Whisk the egg, egg yolks, and remaining sugar in a bowl until fluffy. Pour in the hot milk a little at a time, whisking constantly.

3 Return to the pan and stir over a low heat until the mixture thickens enough to coat the back of the spoon. Leave to cool completely, then chill thoroughly. Strain on to the aubergine, and whisk until smooth. Pour into an ice-cream maker and freeze-churn according to the manufacturer's instructions.

Preparation time
50 minutes, plus 10–13 hours freezing time

Serves 6

Nutritional notes
kcalories 610; protein 7g; carbohydrate 86g; total fat 28g, of which saturated fat 16g; fibre 0.5g; sodium 86mg

BREAKFASTS & BRUNCHES

WHAT BETTER WAY to start the day than with a satisfying meal that can be prepared quickly, then savoured slowly? Here are a few ideas for some appetizing, energy-giving breakfasts and brunches. Mexican scrambled eggs, vegetarian kedgeree,

Blueberry Pancakes, French toast, and fruit-filled popovers are just a few of the international flavours in this section. I like to combine sweet dishes with savoury and spicy ones to create an interesting, full-blown brunch spread.

SIMPLE HUEVOS RANCHEROS

KEY INGREDIENTS

Black beans are shiny, black, kidney-shaped beans, often used in Mexican cookery

Avocado is a soft, pear-shaped fruit, rich in oils and vitamins

Fresh coriander is a very popular herb with a strong flavour

Soured cream has a piquant taste and is excellent in dressings and creamy dips

Tomatoes have a wonderful, sweet flavour and are indispensable as a salsa ingredient

Limes are sour, almost perfumed, citrus fruit, and their juice gives a distinct taste to sauces and salsas

Corn tortillas are made from cornmeal and are usually served deep-fried with a variety of fillings

*O*ne of the classics of Mexican cooking, this can be as soothing or as spicy as you like, depending on how many chillies you add to the sauce. My preference is for a fairly substantial amount of chilli. Cook the beans the night before to save time the following morning.

INGREDIENTS

vegetable oil, for deep-frying

4 corn tortillas

75g (2¾oz) black beans, soaked overnight and cooked (see page 41), then mashed

4 eggs

1 avocado, peeled and diced

4 tbsp soured cream

salt and freshly ground pepper

FOR THE SALSA

150g (5½oz) tomatoes, chopped

½ small onion, chopped

½ garlic clove, crushed

1 small red chilli, finely chopped

1 tbsp chopped fresh coriander, plus leaves, to garnish

2 tbsp lime juice

1 tbsp maple syrup

4 tbsp olive oil

drop Tabasco

1 For the salsa, mix together all the ingredients in a bowl and leave to marinate for up to 30 minutes before using.

2 Heat the vegetable oil in a pan. When hot, deep-fry the corn tortillas for 30 seconds until golden and crispy. Transfer to a plate and keep warm. Heat a little more oil in a separate frying pan and fry the black beans for 1 minute, over a high heat, stirring; set aside and keep warm. Finally, fry the eggs.

3 Place a tortilla on each plate, spoon a generous portion of black beans on top, then add a fried egg. Scatter some diced avocado over each egg. Spoon a little soured cream on top, drizzle the salsa around, then season. Garnish with coriander.

Preparation & cooking time
1½–2 hours, plus overnight soaking time, plus 30 minutes marinating time

Serves 4

Nutritional notes
kcalories 591; protein 19g; carbohydrate 48g; total fat 37g, of which saturated fat 9g; fibre 3g; sodium 379mg

SWEET POPOVERS WITH SPICED FRUIT COMPOTE

The fruit compote and batter for this recipe can be prepared the night before, then kept in the refrigerator. All you have to do in the morning is to cook the popovers and enjoy a healthy, relaxing breakfast.

INGREDIENTS

175g (6oz) plain flour, sifted

pinch salt

1 tbsp caster sugar

2 eggs

300ml (½ pint) milk

40g (1½oz) unsalted butter, melted

4 tsp vegetable oil

FOR THE COMPOTE

2 tbsp maple syrup

1 cinnamon stick

2 cloves

zest and juice of 2 oranges

100g (3½oz) ready-to-eat dried apricots

100g (3½oz) ready-to-eat dried figs

100g (3½oz) ready-to-eat dried prunes

2 tbsp sultanas

25g (1oz) pine nuts, toasted

icing sugar, to dust

crème fraîche, to serve

1 Beat together the flour, salt, sugar, eggs, milk, and butter, until the mixture forms a batter. Leave to rest for 20 minutes.

2 Meanwhile, for the compote, place the maple syrup, cinnamon, and cloves in a pan with 450ml (16fl oz) water. Add the orange zest and juice, and the apricots, figs, and prunes. Bring to the boil, then reduce the heat, and simmer for 10 minutes before stirring in the sultanas.

3 Lift out the fruit and spices, and set aside. Heat the juices over a medium heat until light and syrupy. Remove from the heat, return the fruit to the syrup, discard the spices, and add the pine nuts. Cool in the pan.

4 Pour 1 teaspoon of oil into each section of a four-hole muffin tray and heat in the oven for 3 minutes. Divide the batter between the four holes. Bake for 15 minutes. Reduce the heat to 180°C/350°F/Gas 4 and cook for 10 minutes more until the popovers are golden and puffy. Fill each one with the compote, then dust with icing sugar. Serve with a generous spoonful of crème fraîche.

Oven preheated to 200°C/400°F/Gas 6

Preparation & cooking time 1 hour

Serves 4

Nutritional notes kcalories 697; protein 15g; carbohydrate 89g; total fat 34g, of which saturated fat 12g; fibre 6g; sodium 291mg

BLUEBERRY PANCAKES WITH MAPLE SYRUP

This is the ultimate deluxe version of that great American breakfast staple — buttermilk pancakes. Stack them high on top of each other, American-diner style, and pour over a generous portion of maple syrup. Make sure that you buy the genuine article, not maple-flavour syrup, which is a synthetic concoction.

INGREDIENTS

125g (4½oz) plain flour

2 tsp caster sugar

1 tsp baking powder

½ tsp salt

250ml (9fl oz) milk or buttermilk

40g (1½oz) unsalted butter, melted

1 egg, lightly beaten

50g (1¾oz) pecan nuts, roughly chopped

75g (2¾oz) fresh blueberries, plus extra, to garnish

vegetable oil, for frying

FOR THE SYRUP

150ml (¼ pint) maple syrup

1 tbsp ground cinnamon

1 Combine the dry ingredients in a mixing bowl. Make a well in the centre, and add the milk, butter, and egg. Gradually fold in the dry ingredients, then whisk until the mixture forms a smooth batter. Cover and leave to rest for 1 hour. Mix in the pecan nuts and blueberries.

2 Lightly brush a frying pan with oil. Heat the oil over a high heat, then pour a small ladleful of batter into the pan. Swirl to coat the pan with the batter, and cook for 1–2 minutes on each side. Remove and keep warm. Repeat with the remaining batter to make 12 pancakes.

3 Heat the maple syrup and cinnamon in a pan. Bring to the boil, reduce the heat, then simmer for 2 minutes. Leave to cool. Arrange three pancakes on each plate. Garnish each plate with blueberries, and serve with the cinnamon-infused maple syrup poured over the top.

⏱ **Preparation & cooking time**
25 minutes, plus 1 hour resting time

◎ **Serves 4**

♡ **Nutritional notes**
kcalories 559; protein 9g; carbohydrate 60g; total fat 33g, of which saturated fat 10g; fibre 2g; sodium 285mg

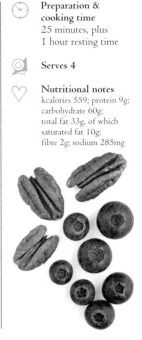

STUFFED FRENCH TOAST

French toast is a great comfort food, but sandwiched together with summer berries and crème fraîche it also makes an elegant brunch dish. You could serve this as a dessert, too.

INGREDIENTS

2 eggs

150ml (¼ pint) single cream or milk

1 tbsp caster sugar

zest of ½ orange

¼ tsp ground cinnamon

4 slices white bread

50g (1¾oz) unsalted butter

crème fraîche or ricotta, to serve

FOR THE FILLING

100g (3½oz) fresh raspberries, puréed

icing sugar, to taste, plus extra, to dust

150g (5½oz) selection summer berries (raspberries, strawberries, and blackberries)

1 For the filling, put the raspberry purée in a pan, and stir in a little icing sugar, to taste. Add the other berries, and cook over a low heat for 15 minutes until the fruit just begins to soften.

2 Beat together the eggs, cream, sugar, orange zest, and cinnamon in a shallow dish. Dip each slice of bread in the egg mixture until soaked through.

3 Heat the butter in a frying pan over a medium heat until sizzling. Fry the bread slices for 2–3 minutes on each side until lightly browned. Remove each slice from the pan and cut in half diagonally.

4 Place half a slice of toast on each serving plate. Divide the warmed summer fruit between them and add a spoonful of crème fraîche to each. Top with the remaining half slices of toast and dust generously with icing sugar. Serve immediately.

⏱ **Preparation & cooking time**
30 minutes

◎ **Serves 4**

♡ **Nutritional notes**
kcalories 351; protein 11g; carbohydrate 30g; total fat 22g, of which saturated fat 13g; fibre 2g; sodium 373mg

SOY WAFFLES WITH PLUM COMPOTE

You will need a waffle iron for this recipe. If you do not have one, however, you could make pancakes with the batter instead, and sandwich the pancakes together with the compote and cream cheese, in the same way as the waffles.

INGREDIENTS

225g (8oz) plain flour

1 tbsp baking powder

½ tsp salt

1 tbsp caster sugar

2 eggs, separated

350ml (12fl oz) soya milk

75g (2¾oz) unsalted butter, melted

150ml (¼ pint) cream cheese

icing sugar, to dust

FOR THE PLUM COMPOTE

250g (9oz) ripe plums, halved, stones removed

50g (1¾oz) caster sugar

1 cinnamon stick

drop vanilla extract

1 For the plum compote, place the plums, sugar, cinnamon, and vanilla extract in a pan, and cover with water so that the fruit are just submerged. Bring to the boil, reduce the heat, and simmer gently, stirring occasionally, for about 30 minutes until the plums are plump and tender. Taste the resulting liquid and adjust the sugar to taste. Allow to cool and discard the cinnamon stick.

2 For the waffles, sift the flour, baking powder, salt, and sugar into a bowl. In a separate bowl, lightly beat the egg yolks and milk, then stir in the butter. Make a well in the centre of the dry ingredients and pour in the egg mixture. Whisk together to form a smooth batter.

3 Beat the egg whites until stiff and gently fold into the batter with a metal spoon. Use the batter to cook eight waffles as instructed on your waffle iron.

4 To serve, place one waffle on each serving plate, top with the plum compote and a dollop of cream cheese, place another waffle on top, then dust liberally with icing sugar.

Preparation & cooking time
1¼ hours

Serves 4

Nutritional notes
kcalories 665; protein 14g; carbohydrate 70g; total fat 39g, of which saturated fat 23g; fibre 3g; sodium 927mg

LANESBOROUGH GRANOLA

This is made regularly for our guests at The Lanesborough hotel in London and is always popular. Vary it by adding different nuts, sunflower or pumpkin seeds, or a touch of ground mixed spice or nutmeg. You could also stir in raisins or other dried fruit once you have broken up the granola.

INGREDIENTS

50g (1¾oz) unsalted butter

50g (1¾oz) brown sugar

4 tbsp honey

2 tbsp golden syrup

4 drops vanilla extract

75g (2¾oz) flaked almonds

75g (2¾oz) pecan nuts, coarsely chopped

25g (1oz) pistachio nuts (optional)

375g (13oz) rolled oats

25g (1oz) desiccated coconut

1 Heat the butter in a large pan, add the sugar, honey, golden syrup, and vanilla extract, and bring to the boil.

2 Reduce the heat. Stir in the nuts, oats, and coconut. Pour the mixture on to a large baking sheet and spread it out evenly. Bake for 20–25 minutes until golden, turning the mixture regularly with a wooden spoon.

3 Turn out the mixture on to a clean work surface and leave for about 1 hour to go cold and hard, turning occasionally.

4 Cover the granola with a clean tea towel and bash it with a kitchen hammer or rolling pin to break it up into fairly small pieces. Store in an airtight container at room temperature for up to 4 weeks.

Oven preheated to
190°C/375°F/Gas 5

Preparation & cooking time
40 minutes, plus 1 hour cooling time

Makes 300g (10½oz)

Nutritional notes
kcalories 359; protein 8g; carbohydrate 41g; total fat 20g, of which saturated fat 5g; fibre 4g; sodium 75mg

MY FAVOURITE MUESLI

This is a simple, light start to the morning, worth getting out of bed for, in fact. For a nice variation replace the rolled oats with wheatgerm and use a flavoured yogurt instead of a natural one.

INGREDIENTS

125g (4½oz) rolled oats

150ml (¼ pint) whipping cream

150ml (¼ pint) natural yogurt

2 tbsp honey

3 Granny Smith apples, skin left on, cored and coarsely grated

2 tbsp flaked almonds

2 tbsp lemon juice

selection of fresh fruit (bananas, grapes, strawberries, raspberries), to serve

1 Place the oats in a bowl and cover with boiling water. Cover the bowl loosely with a clean tea towel, and leave to soak overnight at room temperature.

2 The following day, drain the oats thoroughly, mix in the remaining ingredients, place in a bowl, and serve with some fresh fruit of your choice.

Preparation & cooking time
15 minutes, plus overnight soaking time

Serves 4

Nutritional notes
kcalories 446; protein 9g; carbohydrate 54g; total fat 23g, of which saturated fat 10g; fibre 5g; sodium 62mg

EGG KEDGEREE

This is a kedgeree with a difference since it is served at room temperature rather than hot, and brown rice is used instead of white. The rice adds a good, nutty flavour to the dish. The dressing can be made spicier if you wish, according to individual taste.

INGREDIENTS

250g (9oz) long-grain brown rice

1 small cauliflower, cut in small florets

6 spring onions, shredded

200g (7oz) can chickpeas, drained and rinsed

50g (1¾ oz) cashew nuts, toasted

4 hard-boiled eggs, shelled and halved

fresh coriander leaves, to garnish

lemon wedges, to serve

FOR THE DRESSING

1 tsp curry paste

5 tbsp vegetable oil

2 tbsp chopped fresh coriander

2.5cm (1 inch) piece fresh root ginger, grated

juice of 1 lemon

1 Cook the brown rice in a large pan of boiling water for 20–25 minutes until tender. Drain it well, then rinse under cold, running water and drain again.

2 Cook the cauliflower for 5 minutes in boiling, salted water until just tender. Drain and refresh in cold water. Place the rice and cauliflower in a bowl. Add the spring onions, chickpeas, and cashew nuts, and mix well.

3 For the dressing, blend together all the ingredients, then toss with the rice. Transfer to a salad bowl and arrange the eggs on top. Garnish with fresh coriander, add the lemon wedges, and serve at room temperature.

Preparation & cooking time
45 minutes

Serves 4

Nutritional notes
kcalories 626; protein 19g; carbohydrate 64g; total fat 34g, of which saturated fat 5g; fibre 5g; sodium 197mg

LEEK & BEAN HASH WITH CORIANDER MOJO

Take your time to prepare this dish on a lazy Sunday morning and serve it when your appetite has picked up. You will find that this substantial vegetable hash, with its chilli and coriander topping, makes a memorable brunch dish. If you prefer, you can make one large hash and slice it when cooked.

INGREDIENTS

450g (1lb) large baking potatoes, baked in their skins

4 tbsp olive oil

4 medium leeks, washed and shredded

1 garlic clove, crushed

150g (5½oz) red kidney beans, soaked overnight and cooked (see page 41)

½ tsp ground coriander

50g (1¼oz) Cheddar

1 egg, beaten

1 tbsp cornflour

salt and freshly ground pepper

freshly grated nutmeg

fresh coriander leaves, to garnish

FOR THE MOJO

4 tbsp chopped fresh coriander

350g (12oz) ripe yellow tomatoes, chopped

1 small red onion, chopped

1 green chilli, deseeded and chopped

1 tbsp red wine vinegar

1 tbsp lime juice

1 For the mojo, combine all the ingredients in a bowl and chill in the refrigerator until required.

2 Scoop out the flesh of the potatoes and crush with a fork. Discard the skins. Heat half the olive oil in a frying pan and sauté the leeks and garlic over a medium heat for 5 minutes until soft and lightly browned. Add the kidney beans and cook for 2–3 minutes.

3 Remove from the heat. Mix in the potato, coriander, and Cheddar. Season with salt, pepper, and nutmeg. Transfer to a bowl. Mix in the egg and cornflour, then cover and chill for 30 minutes.

4 Form the mixture into eight patties. Heat the remaining oil in a frying pan and fry the patties over a high heat for 6 minutes on each side until golden. Serve two per person, with the mojo on the side. Garnish with coriander.

Preparation & cooking time
2½ hours, plus overnight soaking time

Serves 4

Nutritional notes
kcalories 638; protein 24g; carbohydrate 100g; total fat 19g, of which saturated fat 5g; fibre 15g; sodium 251mg

PERSIAN BAKED EGGS

Guaranteed to wake you up, this spicy egg and tomato dish can be on the table in 20 minutes. Serve with plenty of bread for mopping up the delicious juices.

INGREDIENTS

6 tbsp vegetable oil

2 garlic cloves, crushed

2 green chillies, deseeded and chopped

750g (1lb 10oz) tomatoes, skinned, deseeded, and finely chopped (see page 39)

4 eggs

salt

4 tbsp chopped fresh coriander, to garnish

pitta bread, to serve

1 Heat the oil in an ovenproof frying pan, add the garlic and chillies, and sweat for 4–5 minutes over a medium heat. Add the chopped tomatoes and cook over a low heat until they are reduced to half their quantity and are quite pulpy. Season with salt.

2 Reduce the heat, then carefully crack the eggs into four separate areas of the pan without breaking the yolks. Cover the pan with a lid and bake in the oven for 5–6 minutes or until the eggs are cooked to your taste.

3 Place one egg on each of four plates, divide the tomato mixture between them, and garnish with coriander. Serve with some warmed pitta bread on the side.

Oven preheated to 180°C/350°F/Gas 4

Preparation & cooking time 20 minutes

Serves 4

Nutritional notes
kcalories 336; protein 12g; carbohydrate 20g; total fat 24g, of which saturated fat 4g; fibre 2g; sodium 325mg

EGG QUESADILLAS WITH CHILLI POTATOES

This dish gives a new twist to eggs for breakfast. Here they are served Mexican style, all wrapped up in tortillas, with chilli-spiced potatoes and a delicious yellow tomato salsa.

INGREDIENTS

4 tbsp oil

150g (5½oz) new potatoes, boiled, peeled, and sliced

1 green chilli, deseeded and very finely chopped

4 spring onions, finely chopped

25g (1oz) butter

4 tbsp double cream

50g (1¼oz) fresh spinach, cooked and finely chopped

3 eggs, beaten

4 flour tortillas

75g (2¼oz) Cheddar, coarsely grated

salt and freshly ground pepper

pinch freshly grated nutmeg

coriander leaves, to garnish

FOR THE SALSA

250g (9oz) yellow tomatoes, quartered

1 shallot, chopped

2 tbsp fresh coriander, chopped

1 green chilli, halved and deseeded

2 tbsp maple syrup

juice of ½ lime

½ garlic clove

1 For the salsa, place all the ingredients in a blender or food processor and blend to a coarse purée. Season, pour into a bowl, and set aside.

2 Heat the oil in a frying pan and sauté the potatoes over a fairly high heat for 5–8 minutes until golden, turning them often. Add the chilli and spring onions, season to taste, remove from the heat, and keep warm.

3 In a large pan, bring the butter and cream to the boil. Reduce the heat, add the spinach and eggs, and cook over a gentle heat, stirring, until you have fluffy scrambled eggs. Add salt, pepper, and nutmeg, to taste.

4 Heat the tortillas in a dry frying pan, over a low heat, for 5–10 seconds on each side. Divide the potatoes and eggs between the tortillas. Sprinkle the Cheddar on top. Roll up each tortilla loosely. Cut in half, place on a bed of salsa, and garnish with coriander.

Preparation & cooking time 40 minutes

Serves 4

Nutritional notes
kcalories 553; protein 17g; carbohydrate 49g; total fat 34g, of which saturated fat 14g; fibre 3g; sodium 520mg

ALFRESCO EATING

COOKING AND EATING OUTDOORS require some special thought. Barbecued food has to stand up to being cooked quickly over an intense heat, while picnic fare must be at its best served cold. Here are some ideas for alliances of vegetables, sauces, and marinades that are accentuated by the wonderful smoky flavours created by chargrilling. There are also recipes for picnic foods, such as savoury pies and pizza with a salad topping. Mix and match the recipes to suit your needs and the occasion.

GRILLED VEGETABLE BARBECUE PITTA PIZZAS

Grilled Vegetable Pitta Pizza

Spinach & Mushroom Pitta Pizza

Fennel & Mozzarella Pitta Pizza

The variations for toppings on these little pizzas are endless. Here are three of my favourites, but make the most of a long, hot summer and experiment with toppings of your own.

INGREDIENTS

1 courgette, sliced
1 red pepper, deseeded and quartered
1 small red onion, thinly sliced
6 large tomatoes, deseeded and chopped
4 tbsp Zhug Relish (see page 67)
1 garlic clove, crushed
125ml (4fl oz) olive oil
8 mini pitta breads
150g (5½oz) feta, coarsely grated
salt and freshly ground pepper

1 Place the courgette, pepper, and onion pieces on skewers that have been soaked in water; baste with oil and season well. Barbecue the vegetables for 25 minutes, turning, until well charred. Remove the skewers.

2 Mix the chopped tomato with the zhug relish. Blend together the garlic and oil and brush over one side of each pitta, then spread with the tomato and zhug relish.

3 Arrange the vegetables on the pittas. Top with feta and barbecue for 2–3 minutes. Wrap loosely in foil and barbecue for 2–3 minutes more. Serve hot.

VARIATIONS

Spinach & Mushroom Pitta Pizzas
Heat 2 tablespoons of olive oil and sauté 4 sliced garlic cloves over a low heat for 8 minutes. Add 75g (2¾oz) sliced button mushrooms and sauté for 3 minutes. Stir in 150g (5½oz) spinach. Add nutmeg and season. Spoon on to the pittas, then top with pine kernels and Parmesan shavings. Barbecue as above.

Fennel & Mozzarella Pitta Pizzas
Slice 2 fennel bulbs thinly; baste with 4 tablespoons of olive oil. Bake at 200°C/400°F/Gas 6 for 3 minutes. Spread 4 tablespoons of Olivada (see page 45) over the pittas, then top with the fennel, 2 thinly sliced courgettes, and 6 sliced sun-dried tomatoes. Brush with olive oil and top with mozzarella. Barbecue as above.

🕐 **Preparation & cooking time**
1 hour

◎ **Serves 4**

♡ **Nutritional notes**
kcalories 671; protein 15g; carbohydrate 53g; total fat 46g, of which saturated fat 11g; fibre 5g; sodium 1020mg

FOIL-GRILLED FETA WITH ONION JAM

Feta has the advantage that it keeps its shape well when grilled, so it is perfect for barbecues. You could alternatively use haloumi, another firm-textured cheese. The onion jam keeps well in the refrigerator for three to four days and can be served as a relish with all sorts of dishes. I like to serve it in sandwiches with a grilled vegetable or a cheese base.

INGREDIENTS

200g (7oz) packet feta

100ml (3½fl oz) olive oil

2 garlic cloves, roughly chopped

1 tsp roughly chopped fresh rosemary

1 tsp roughly chopped fresh thyme

1 tsp roughly chopped fresh oregano

salt and roughly cracked black pepper

FOR THE ONION JAM

4 tbsp olive oil

2 medium red onions, chopped

1 tbsp brown sugar

100ml (3½fl oz) sherry or red wine vinegar

pinch ground cumin

1 Cut the feta into four equal slices and place in a large, shallow dish in one layer. Pour the oil over the feta, scatter the garlic and herbs on top, and season with salt (not too much because the feta is already quite salty) and some roughly cracked black pepper. Cover and leave to marinate in a cool place for up to 4 hours.

2 Meanwhile, for the onion jam, heat the oil over a low heat, add the onion, and cook slowly for 10–12 minutes until soft and tender. Stir in the remaining ingredients and cook for a further 30 minutes, stirring occasionally, until the onions become soft and syrupy. Remove from the heat and set aside.

3 Remove the feta from the marinade. Lay four pieces of foil, each about 25cm (10 inches) square, out on a table. Divide the onion jam equally between the squares. Top each with a slice of feta and pour 1 tablespoon of the marinade over each piece of feta.

4 Bring the corners of the foil together and fold the top over to encase the onions and cheese. Place the parcels on a hot barbecue and cook for 4–5 minutes until the cheese just begins to soften. Transfer to individual plates. Allow guests to open their own pouches so that they can savour the heady aroma that is released.

Preparation & cooking time
1¼ hours, plus 4 hours marinating time

Serves 4

Nutritional notes
kcalories 497; protein 9g; carbohydrate 11g; total fat 46g, of which saturated fat 12g; fibre 1g; sodium 824mg

LENTIL BURGERS WITH TOMATO RAITA

I am not usually impressed with vegetarian dishes that imitate meat, but these burgers are in a class of their own. Spiced with chilli, cumin, and coriander, and served with a cooling tomato and yogurt sauce, this is one of those dishes that tends to be enthusiastically consumed by non-vegetarians, too. Twice-cooked Spicy Potato Skins (see page 150) make an excellent accompaniment to this dish.

INGREDIENTS

6 tbsp vegetable oil

175g (6oz) Puy lentils, cooked (see page 41)

1 green chilli, deseeded and chopped

1 garlic clove, crushed

3 spring onions, finely sliced

1 tbsp ground cumin

½ tbsp ground coriander

4 tbsp chickpea flour

1 small egg, beaten

4 soft baps

1 avocado

juice of ½ lemon

salt and freshly ground pepper

FOR THE TOMATO RAITA

6 tbsp natural yogurt

2 tomatoes, cubed

½ tbsp chopped fresh mint

1 tbsp chopped fresh coriander

2 spring onions, finely sliced

1 Heat 4 tablespoons of vegetable oil in a frying pan. Add the lentils, chilli, and garlic, and fry for 2–3 minutes over a medium heat, stirring. Add the onions and spices, and season. Stir in the chickpea flour and cook for 2–3 minutes. Place the mixture in a bowl and leave to cool.

2 When cool, mix in the egg and stir well to bind all the ingredients together. Cover and refrigerate for 1 hour.

3 Meanwhile, for the raita, blend together all the ingredients in a bowl and season. Cover and leave to chill in the refrigerator until ready to serve.

4 Take the lentil mixture out of the refrigerator and shape into small burgers or patties. Brush them all over with the remaining oil and grill on a hot barbecue for 3–4 minutes on each side until well browned and sizzling. Alternatively, fry the burgers over a high heat for 3–4 minutes on each side.

5 Cut the baps in half and toast the sliced side for a few minutes on the barbecue. Peel and stone the avocado and slice it thinly. Sprinkle the slices with a little lemon juice to prevent them from discolouring.

6 Place a good spoonful of raita over the base of each toasted bap, put a lentil burger on top with a few slices of avocado, then top with the other half of the bap and serve.

Preparation & cooking time
1 hour 50 minutes

Serves 4

Nutritional notes
kcalories 694; protein 24g;
carbohydrate 82g;
total fat 33g, of which
saturated fat 6g;
fibre 6g; sodium 812mg

PEPPERED MUSHROOM & TOFU SATAY

Mushrooms and tofu work well together on kebabs because they soak up the spicy flavours of the marinade. Here they are served with a peanut vinaigrette, but if you prefer a more traditional satay sauce try the Asian Peanut Dip (see page 156).

Peppered Mushroom & Tofu Satay

INGREDIENTS

350g (12oz) firm tofu, cut in 2.5cm (1 inch) chunks

12 large flat mushrooms, quartered

salt

1 tsp mixed peppercorns, cracked

FOR THE MARINADE

1 stick lemongrass, chopped

1 tbsp ground cumin

1 tbsp ground turmeric

2 garlic cloves

5cm (2 inch) piece fresh root ginger, grated

2 shallots

½ tsp ground cinnamon

75g (2½oz) demerara sugar

150ml (¼ pint) peanut oil

FOR THE PEANUT VINAIGRETTE

6 tbsp rice wine vinegar

1 tbsp chopped fresh coriander

3 fresh mint leaves, chopped

½ garlic clove, crushed

½ red chilli, deseeded and finely chopped

25g (1oz) dry roasted peanuts, chopped

1 tbsp maple syrup

soy sauce, to taste

1 Thread the tofu and the mushroom pieces alternately on to eight wooden skewers that have been soaked in water. Lay the skewers in a shallow dish. Sprinkle with the salt and the cracked, mixed peppercorns.

2 For the marinade, place all the ingredients in a blender or food processor and blend to a fine pulp. Pour the marinade over the tofu and mushrooms to coat well. Cover and leave to marinate in the refrigerator for 12 hours.

3 When ready to serve, remove the skewered vegetables from the dish and pat away the excess marinade with kitchen paper.

Place the skewers on the hottest part of the barbecue and cook for 5–8 minutes. Turn the skewers occasionally.

4 Meanwhile, for the peanut vinaigrette, whisk together all the ingredients, and season to taste. To serve, spoon a little peanut vinaigrette on to four plates and place two skewers of vegetables on each plate.

VARIATION

Aubergine, Potato & Squash Satay
Cook 200g (7oz) large new potatoes in boiling, salted water for 15–20 minutes until just tender. Drain, and leave to cool. Peel the potatoes, cut in large chunks, and cut 8 baby aubergines in half, lengthways. Arrange the potatoes and aubergines with 8 mixed yellow and green pattypan squash in alternate pieces on the skewers. Place the kebabs in 1 quantity of prepared marinade (see left). Leave to marinate for 12 hours. Cook on a hot barbecue for 10–15 minutes, turning regularly, until the vegetables are tender. Chop 1 green chilli and sprinkle it over the kebabs. Serve with peanut vinaigrette (see above).

Preparation & cooking time
35–40 minutes, plus 12 hours marinating time

Serves 4

Nutritional notes
kcalories 546; protein 11g; carbohydrate 27g; total fat 45g, of which saturated fat 9g; fibre 1g; sodium 233mg

Aubergine, Potato & Squash Satay

VEGETABLE SHASHLIKS ON TABBOULEH

You can use just about any vegetable to make these kebabs, but for maximum visual appeal it is best to go for a good selection of colours. I first prepared this dish for my television series The Green Gourmet and it was served to shoppers when we were filming on location in West London.

INGREDIENTS

1 cauliflower, cut in florets and blanched
3 peppers (1 red, 1 green, 1 yellow), cut in 2.5cm (1 inch) chunks
2 courgettes, cut in chunks
100g (3½oz) button mushrooms
1 large red onion, cut in wedges

FOR THE TABBOULEH

325g (11½oz) bulgar wheat, soaked in water for 45 minutes and drained
3 tbsp chopped fresh parsley
2 onions, chopped
2 tbsp chopped fresh mint
½ cucumber, chopped
100ml (3½fl oz) olive oil
juice of 3 lemons
3 tomatoes, skinned, deseeded, and chopped (see page 39)
1 quantity marinade (see below)

1 Thread alternate pieces of vegetables decoratively on to eight wooden skewers that have been soaked in water. Place them in a shallow dish.

2 Prepare the marinade of your choice (see below). Pour the marinade over the vegetables. Cover and marinate for 1 hour.

3 Meanwhile, for the tabbouleh, place the bulgar wheat in a tea towel and squeeze out any excess water. Transfer the bulgar wheat to a bowl, add the remaining ingredients, and mix well. Season to taste and place in a flat serving dish.

4 Take the skewered vegetables from the marinade, let any excess drip off, then grill on a hot barbecue for 10–12 minutes, turning regularly, until lightly charred on all sides and cooked through. Arrange the shashliks on the tabbouleh.

5 Gently heat the marinade in a small pan until just before boiling. Pour the marinade over the kebabs to serve. If using the Spicy Yogurt Marinade, do not heat the marinade.

Preparation & cooking time
50 minutes, plus 1 hour for the marinade, plus 1 hour marinating time

Serves 4

Nutritional notes
kcalories 1001; protein 18g; carbohydrate 87g; total fat 66g, of which saturated fat 9g; fibre 8g; sodium 198mg

Vegetable Shashliks

VEGETABLE SHASHLIK MARINADES

Greek Marinade

Middle Eastern Marinade

GREEK MARINADE
Whisk together 100ml (3½fl oz) olive oil and the juice of 2 lemons. Stir in 2 crushed garlic cloves, 2 finely chopped onions, 1 bay leaf, and 1 tablespoon of chopped fresh oregano. Leave to infuse for 1 hour, then use as directed above.

MIDDLE EASTERN MARINADE
Blend 150ml (¼ pint) olive oil with 2 tablespoons of tomato purée, the juice of 1 lemon, 1 crushed garlic clove, 1 grated onion, and a pinch each of saffron and ground cumin. Mix well, leave to infuse for 1 hour, then use as directed above.

MOROCCAN MARINADE
Blend 150ml (¼ pint) olive oil with 1 tablespoon of canned harissa, 1 tablespoon of caraway seeds, a pinch each of cumin and turmeric, and 1 crushed garlic clove. Mix well, then leave to infuse for 1 hour. Use as directed above.

SPICY YOGURT MARINADE
Blend 150ml (¼ pint) natural yogurt with 2 tablespoons curry paste, ½ teaspoon ground turmeric, and 2.5cm (1 inch) piece fresh root ginger, grated. Leave to infuse for 1 hour, then use as directed above, but do not heat this marinade before using.

HOT CHILLI-BASTED CORN ON THE COB

Corn on the cob is one of the great treats of summer, even more so when spiked with lots of chilli and my favourite herb – coriander.

INGREDIENTS
6 tbsp olive oil
2 tbsp chopped fresh coriander
1 tbsp tomato purée
2 tbsp hot chilli sauce
4 corn on the cob, husks removed
butter, to serve
fresh coriander leaves, to garnish

1 For the marinade, whisk the oil, coriander, tomato purée, and chilli sauce in a bowl.

2 Cut each corn on the cob widthways into three and blanch in a pan of boiling water for about 2 minutes. Drain, then place in a shallow dish. Pour the marinade over the corn to coat well. Cover and leave for 2 hours.

3 Grill the corn on a hot barbecue for 30–40 minutes, regularly turning and brushing with the marinade. Serve hot, topped with butter or more of the marinade. Garnish with coriander.

Preparation & cooking time
50 minutes, plus 2 hours marinating time

Serves 4

Nutritional notes
kcalories 338; protein 5g; carbohydrate 24g; total fat 25g, of which saturated fat 7g; fibre 2g; sodium 401mg

TWICE-COOKED SPICY POTATO SKINS

I have never understood why some people throw away the skins from their jacket potatoes: for me this is the tastiest part. When cooked in an Asian-style spice mix, deep-fried potato skins are just irresistible. Try dipping these into soured cream or Tomato Raita (see page 147).

INGREDIENTS
6 large baking potatoes
50g (1¾oz) chickpea flour or plain flour
1 tsp turmeric
1 tsp chilli powder
½ tsp garam masala
salt
vegetable oil, for frying

1 Prick the potatoes all over with a fork and bake for 1–1¼ hours, depending on their size, until cooked through. Leave until cool enough to handle.

2 Cut each potato in half lengthways and scoop out most of the flesh, leaving a 5mm (¼ inch) shell.

3 Cut each skin in half again lengthways. Mix together the flour, spices, and salt, to taste. Dip the skins in the flour to coat.

4 Heat the oil in a deep-fat fryer or large pan until hot. Deep-fry the potato skins for 3–4 minutes or until they are crisp. Drain on kitchen paper, season with salt, and serve.

Oven preheated to
200°C/400°F/Gas 6

Preparation & cooking time
1½–2 hours

Serves 4

Nutritional notes
kcalories 311; protein 6g; carbohydrate 38g; total fat 16g, of which saturated fat 2g; fibre 4g; sodium 116mg

CHAR-BAKED TOMATOES WITH GARLIC

Everything tastes good when it has been cooked on a barbecue and for me tomatoes are no exception. Here basil, garlic, and an open grill combine to give an extra flavour dimension.

INGREDIENTS
4 tbsp olive oil
1 garlic clove, crushed
2 tbsp chopped fresh basil
pinch of caster sugar
8 ripe, but firm tomatoes, halved vertically
salt and freshly ground pepper

1 In a bowl, mix together the olive oil, garlic, basil, sugar, and seasoning until well blended.

2 Place the tomato halves cut-side up on a baking sheet and drizzle the garlic and basil oil over them. Transfer the tomatoes on to a hot barbecue and grill for about 8 minutes until charred and softened. Serve hot.

Preparation & cooking time
15 minutes

Serves 4

Nutritional notes
kcalories 131; protein 1g; carbohydrate 6g; total fat 12g, of which saturated fat 2g; fibre 2g; sodium 114mg

GREEN OLIVE & ONION BREAD

Olives and onions make this loaf hearty enough to serve as the centrepiece of a simple outdoor meal. It is best eaten fresh from the oven, but will still taste great the next day. It is excellent served with cheese.

INGREDIENTS

4 tbsp olive oil, plus extra, to grease

2 onions, chopped

450g (1lb) strong plain white flour

225g (8oz) plain wholemeal flour, plus extra, to dust

7g (¼oz) sachet easy-blend yeast

2 tsp salt

450ml (16fl oz) tepid water

200g (7oz) pitted green olives, chopped

1 Heat 1 tablespoon of the olive oil in a pan and fry the onions for 5 minutes until softened; cool.

2 Place both flours in a mixing bowl and stir in the yeast and salt. Pour in 2 tablespoons of oil and slowly add enough tepid water to make a soft, but not sticky, dough. You may need to add a little more flour or water to achieve the right consistency.

3 Turn the dough on to a lightly floured work surface and knead until smooth and elastic.

Place the dough in a large, lightly greased bowl, cover with a clean cloth, and leave in a warm place for 1 hour until doubled in size.

4 When risen, knock back the dough, turn it on to a lightly floured surface, and knead again for 1 minute. Next, add the cooled onion, the remaining oil, and the olives, kneading again for 2 minutes to combine and distribute the ingredients evenly.

5 Shape the dough into a free-form round loaf, place on an oiled baking sheet, and cover with a clean cloth. Leave in a warm place to rise for 25–30 minutes until doubled in size.

6 Remove the cloth and bake the loaf for 45 minutes. Tap the base to see if it is cooked: it should sound hollow. If it does not, place the loaf back in the oven and bake for a few more minutes until it is done. Leave to cool on a wire rack.

Oven preheated to
180°C/350°F/Gas 4

Preparation & cooking time
1¼ hours, plus 1½ hours proving time

Serves 4

Nutritional notes
kcalories 564; protein 15g; carbohydrate 91g; total fat 18g, of which saturated fat 3g; fibre 6g; sodium 2114mg

LIME-GRILLED FRUIT ON LEMONGRASS STICKS

Barbecuing fruit on lemongrass passes a delicate citrus flavour on to the fruit. You may want to vary the fruit, but this is an exotic, yet simple, kebab to impress your guests. You may need to sharpen the ends of the lemongrass sticks to spear the fruit.

INGREDIENTS

¼ melon of your choice (canteloupe or ogen), deseeded and cut in 2.5cm (1 inch) chunks

1 papaya, cut in 2.5cm (1 inch) chunks

2 plums, halved and stones removed

1 nectarine, cut in 2.5cm (1 inch) chunks

12 strawberries

4 sticks lemongrass, tips sharpened

tangy fruit sorbet, to serve (optional)

FOR THE MARINADE

4 tbsp freshly squeezed lime juice

3 tbsp peanut oil

2 tbsp maple syrup

2 tbsp vodka (optional)

1 Whisk together the marinade ingredients. Place all the fruit in a bowl and pour over the marinade. Cover and leave for up to 1 hour in a cool place.

2 Remove the fruit from the marinade with a slotted spoon, then spear in alternate chunks on to the lemongrass sticks. Reserve the marinade.

3 Grill the fruit on the barbecue for 5–8 minutes, turning and basting them regularly with the marinade until golden and lightly singed. Serve hot from the grill with a tangy fruit sorbet, if desired.

Preparation & cooking time
20 minutes, plus 1 hour marinating time

Serves 4

Nutritional notes
kcalories 269; protein 2g; carbohydrate 45g; total fat 8g, of which saturated fat 2g; fibre 2g; sodium 39mg

CARROT & BEAN PIE WITH THYME CREAM

Lots of fresh thyme and Dijon mustard lift the flavour of simple vegetables in this substantial pie. Served cold, it is a good choice for a picnic or buffet party, and cuts into colourful slices.

INGREDIENTS

butter, to grease
675g (1lb 8oz) Shortcrust Pastry (see page 42)
6 large carrots
400g (14oz) French beans
300ml (½ pint) double cream
2 tbsp Dijon mustard
4 tbsp fresh thyme leaves
2 tbsp cornflour, mixed to a paste with 4 tbsp cold water
6 small eggs, beaten
salt and freshly ground pepper

1 Lightly grease a 22cm (8½ inch) springform cake tin. Roll out two-thirds of the pastry on a lightly floured work surface and use to line the tin.

2 Cook the carrots whole in boiling, salted water for 10 minutes until tender; drain. Slice lengthways into 3mm (⅛ inch) thick slices. In a separate pan, cook the beans in boiling, salted water for 4 minutes until al dente. Refresh in cold water, then pat dry.

3 In a milk pan, bring the cream, mustard, and thyme to the boil. Stir in the cornflour paste to thicken the mixture. Remove from the heat, cool, then mix in the eggs.

4 Lay half the carrots in the pastry case, then lay all the beans over them, and top with the remaining carrots. Press each layer down lightly, season, and pour over a little thyme cream before adding the next layer.

5 Roll out the remaining pastry to cover the pie. Brush the edges with water and press down to seal. Bake for 1¼ hours until golden. Leave to rest for 10–15 minutes before slicing.

Oven preheated to 190°C/375°F/Gas 5

Preparation & cooking time 2 hours, plus 40 minutes for the pastry

Serves 10

Nutritional notes kcalories 874; protein 14g; carbohydrate 71g; total fat 61g, of which saturated fat 37g; fibre 4g; sodium 351mg

VEGETABLE PICNIC CAKE

A cake made with ingredients that are usually associated with savoury dishes is not unusual — consider how popular carrot cake has become. Courgettes, sun-dried tomatoes, and pine kernels all have a subtle sweetness, and combine to produce a moist, flavoursome cake. Salting the courgettes extracts the excess moisture.

INGREDIENTS

175g (6oz) courgettes, coarsely grated
4 eggs
150g (5½oz) unsalted butter, melted
1 tsp vanilla extract
175g (6oz) caster sugar
200g (7oz) plain flour
1 tsp salt, plus extra, for salting
1½ tsp baking powder
50g (1¾oz) sun-dried tomatoes, sliced
50g (1¾oz) pine nuts
zest of 1 lemon

1 Place the courgettes in a bowl, sprinkle with salt, and leave to stand for 10 minutes. Rinse the courgettes under cold, running water, then wrap in a clean cloth and gently squeeze dry; set aside.

2 In a blender or food processor, blend together the eggs, melted butter, vanilla, and sugar. Mix together the flour, salt, and baking powder in a separate bowl, then add to the egg mixture and blend until smooth. Place in a bowl and add the courgettes, sun-dried tomatoes, pine nuts, and lemon zest.

3 Butter and lightly flour a 450g (1lb) loaf tin. Pour the mixture into the tin, level the top with a spatula, and bake for 10–12 minutes. Reduce the oven temperature to 180°C/350°F/Gas 4 and bake for a further 50 minutes. When cooked, a fine skewer inserted into the middle of the cake should come out clean. Cool on a wire rack. Serve cold.

Oven preheated to 200°C/400°F/Gas 6

Preparation & cooking time 1½ hours

Serves 8

Nutritional notes
kcalories 394; protein 7g; carbohydrate 43g; total fat 22g, of which saturated fat 12g; fibre 0.2g; sodium 443mg

SPRING VEGETABLE QUINOA

A South American grain, quinoa is packed full of essential nutrients. Its flavour is quite bland, but here it is perked up with a herby, onion-scented dressing to make a healthy and refreshing salad.

INGREDIENTS

200g (7oz) quinoa grain
100g (3½oz) courgettes, thinly sliced
100g (3½oz) sugar-snap peas
75g (2¾oz) frozen peas, defrosted
75g (2¾oz) frozen broad beans, blanched and peeled
125g (4½oz) can sweetcorn kernels
1 red onion, finely chopped
1 stick lemongrass, finely chopped
FOR THE DRESSING
150ml (¼ pint) olive oil
1 clove garlic, crushed
1 tbsp white wine vinegar
1 tbsp chopped fresh coriander
1 tbsp chopped fresh mint
1 tsp ground cumin
salt and freshly ground pepper

1 Place the quinoa in a pan. Cover with cold, salted water, bring to the boil, then simmer for 10–12 minutes. Drain well and leave to cool.

2 Cook the courgettes and sugar-snap peas in boiling, salted water for 2 minutes. Add the peas and beans, and boil for a further 30 seconds. Refresh in cold water, then drain.

3 Place all of the ingredients for the dressing in a blender or food processor and blend until smooth. Put the drained quinoa, the blanched vegetables, and the sweetcorn in a bowl with the onion, lemongrass, and dressing. Mix the ingredients well and chill in the refrigerator before serving.

Preparation & cooking time 40 minutes

Serves 4

Nutritional notes
kcalories 642; protein 13g; carbohydrate 58g; total fat 41g, of which saturated fat 6g; fibre 4g; sodium 372mg

CRISP ITALIAN TART

This light tart is quick to assemble and looks very attractive with its colourful rows of contrasting vegetables. You could use puff pastry instead of filo pastry, if you prefer.

INGREDIENTS

2 tbsp butter, melted, plus extra, to grease

4 sheets filo pastry, each 20cm x 15cm (8 inches x 6 inches)

1 large courgette

1 large aubergine

4 large plum tomatoes

2 tbsp extra virgin olive oil

1 garlic clove, crushed

1 tsp dried herbes de Provence

salt and freshly ground pepper

1 Lightly grease a 20cm x 15cm (8 inch x 6 inch) shallow baking sheet. Brush each sheet of filo with butter and layer the sheets on top of each other on the baking sheet.

2 Slice the courgette, aubergine, and tomatoes very thinly and place on the pastry, overlapping each other, until all the pastry is covered with the vegetables.

3 Mix together the olive oil and garlic, and brush over the vegetables. Season with salt and pepper and sprinkle the herbes de Provence over the top.

4 Bake for 10–12 minutes until the vegetables are tender and the pastry is cooked. Serve the tart either warm or cold.

Oven preheated to 200°C/400°F/Gas 6

Preparation & cooking time 30 minutes

Serves 4

Nutritional notes kcalories 166; protein 3g; carbohydrate 11g; total fat 12g, of which saturated fat 5g; fibre 2g; sodium 190mg

MIXED SALAD PIZZA WITH ROASTED GARLIC

Piquant, deliciously creamy Gorgonzola paired with sweet, roasted garlic and the bitterness of salad greens make a superb, rich and complex topping for a pizza.

INGREDIENTS

225g (8oz) strong plain flour, plus extra, to dust

½ tsp easy-blend yeast

pinch salt

150ml (¼ pint) tepid water

FOR THE TOPPING

2 tbsp olive oil, plus extra, to grease

4 garlic cloves, roasted, peeled, and mashed (see page 50)

200g (7oz) mixed salad leaves (rocket, endive, iceberg, basil), shredded

75g (2¾oz) raisins, soaked in cold water for 10 minutes, then drained

150g (5½oz) Gorgonzola, grated

1 tbsp freshly grated Parmesan

2 tbsp pine kernels, lightly toasted

1 For the pizza dough, sift the flour into a large bowl, then stir in the yeast and salt. Make a well in the centre of the flour and gradually add the water, mixing the flour in with a wooden spoon to form a soft dough.

2 Knead the dough until smooth and elastic. Place in a lightly oiled bowl, cover with oiled clingfilm, and leave to rise in a warm place for 40 minutes until doubled in size.

3 Meanwhile, for the topping, heat the oil in a frying pan, add the roasted garlic and the shredded salad leaves, and stir-fry for 5 minutes to wilt the leaves.

4 Place the dough on a lightly floured work surface and knock back with your fists. Knead for 2–3 minutes, then roll out to a circle, about 23cm (9 inches) in diameter and 1cm (½ inch) thick. Place on a greased baking sheet.

5 Roll in the edges of the dough to form the crust. Scatter the raisins over the dough, and cover with the garlic and salad leaves. Scatter the Gorgonzola, Parmesan, and pine kernels over the top. Bake for 15–20 minutes until golden.

Oven preheated to 220°C/425°F/Gas 7

Preparation & cooking time 40 minutes, plus 40 minutes proving time

Serves 4

Nutritional notes kcalories 646; protein 24g; carbohydrate 63g; total fat 35g, of which saturated fat 11g; fibre 4g; sodium 611mg

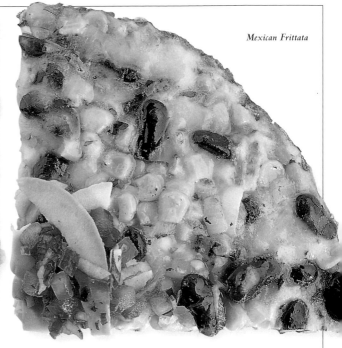

Mixed Salad Pizza with Roasted Garlic

Mexican Frittata

MEXICAN FRITTATA

Flat omelettes, or frittatas, can be filled with all sorts of interesting ingredients – I have gone for a Mexican theme here. The best cooking method is to start the omelette off on the stove, and then transfer it to the oven to cook through, as suggested in this recipe. If you do not have an ovenproof frying pan, simply cook the omelette on the stove until almost done, then place it under a hot grill to set the top.

INGREDIENTS

2 tbsp vegetable oil
1 small onion, diced
1 garlic clove, crushed
150g (5½oz) sweetcorn kernels
100g (3½oz) dried black beans, soaked overnight and cooked (see page 41)
1 tbsp chopped fresh oregano
6 eggs, beaten
2 tbsp unsalted butter
50g (1¼oz) mature Cheddar
salt and freshly ground pepper
crème fraîche, to serve (optional)

FOR THE AVOCADO SALSA

1 avocado, thinly sliced
½ medium onion, chopped
2 tomatoes, chopped
2 tsp chilli sauce
1 tbsp maple syrup
2 tbsp chopped fresh coriander

1 Place all the salsa ingredients in a bowl. Mix well, then set aside to allow the flavours to develop.

2 Heat the oil in an ovenproof frying pan and fry the onion, garlic, sweetcorn kernels, and black beans over a medium heat for 1–2 minutes. Stir in the oregano, then transfer the mixture to a large bowl. Leave to cool, then stir in the eggs and season.

3 Melt the butter in the same pan. When melted, return the egg mixture to the pan and cook for 1–2 minutes over a low heat until set around the edges.

4 Transfer the pan to the oven for 10–12 minutes. When the mixture has set completely, remove the pan from the oven and scatter the cheese over the top. Brown under a hot grill for 1 minute. Divide the frittata into four equal portions and place one portion on four individual plates. Top with the salsa and the crème fraîche, if using.

Oven preheated to 180°C/350°F/Gas 4

Preparation & cooking time 1 hour 50 minutes, plus overnight soaking time

Serves 4

Nutritional notes kcalories 565; protein 24g; carbohydrate 27g; total fat 40g, of which saturated fat 16g; fibre 3g; sodium 396mg

BLACK-EYE BEAN HUMMUS

I must confess that this hummus recipe came about by accident, when I ran out of chickpeas one day. I had no option but to prepare it with black-eye beans; the result was great.

INGREDIENTS

175g (6oz) dried black-eye beans, soaked overnight and cooked (see page 41)

3 garlic cloves, crushed

150ml (¼ pint) tahini (sesame seed paste)

juice of 2–3 lemons

2 tbsp olive oil

1 tbsp chopped fresh parsley, to garnish

pinch paprika, to serve

1 Drain the beans, reserving the cooking liquor, and set aside a tablespoon of beans for garnishing.

2 Purée the beans in a blender or food processor with 2 tablespoons of the reserved cooking liquor. When ground to a coarse paste, add the garlic and tahini and blend together thoroughly. Lastly, pour in the lemon juice and blend until the hummus has a rich, creamy, smooth consistency.

3 Place the hummus in a shallow bowl. To serve, pour the oil over the surface, garnish with the parsley and the reserved beans, and sprinkle the paprika over the top.

Preparation time
1 hour 15 minutes, plus overnight soaking time

Serves 10

Nutritional notes
kcalories 163; protein 7g; carbohydrate 8g; total fat 11g, of which saturated fat 2g; fibre 1g; sodium 10mg

ASIAN PEANUT DIP

Peanut butter provides a useful shortcut when making satay-style sauces; for the best flavour try to find an unsweetened one. Serve this recipe as a dip, or as a sauce for vegetable kebabs.

INGREDIENTS

2 tbsp groundnut or vegetable oil

2 garlic cloves, crushed

1 small red chilli, deseeded and chopped

2 tbsp brown sugar

2 tbsp light soy sauce

175g (6oz) crunchy peanut butter

1 tbsp lemon juice

100ml (3½ fl oz) coconut milk

salt and freshly ground pepper

1 Heat the oil in a medium pan and fry the garlic and chilli for 2–3 minutes over a medium heat, then add the sugar and soy sauce and stir until the sugar is dissolved.

2 Mix in the peanut butter and lemon juice, stir well, and pour in the coconut milk. Bring to the boil, reduce the heat, then simmer, stirring constantly, for about 10 minutes until thickened. Season to taste and serve.

Preparation & cooking time
20–25 minutes

Serves 10

Nutritional notes
kcalories 142; protein 5g; carbohydrate 5g; total fat 12g, of which saturated fat 2g; fibre 1g; sodium 288mg

MOROCCAN PEPPER & WALNUT DIP

This is very similar to the Spanish Romanesco sauce, which is traditionally served with seafood. However, it is very versatile: it can be used as a sauce or dressing for vegetables when thinned with a little cream. I also serve it as a dip with pitta bread or vegetable crudités.

INGREDIENTS

125g (4½oz) walnuts, roasted

1 tbsp cumin seeds

4 red peppers, roasted, peeled, deseeded (see page 39), and cut in strips

1 garlic clove, crushed

1 tbsp lemon juice

2 tbsp olive oil

2 tbsp fresh white breadcrumbs

1 tsp harissa, or to taste

pitta bread, cut in strips, to serve

1 Place the walnuts and cumin in a blender or food processor and blend to a powder. Add the peppers, garlic, and lemon juice to the walnut mixture in the blender and blend to a coarse paste.

2 Add the oil and the breadcrumbs and blend to form a thick, smooth sauce. Add harissa to taste, mix well, and chill for up to 1 hour. Serve with strips of warm pitta bread.

Preparation time
50 minutes, plus 1 hour chilling time

Serves 10

Nutritional notes
kcalories 222; protein 6g; carbohydrate 25g; total fat 12g, of which saturated fat 1g; fibre 2g; sodium 205mg

TRIPLE CLUB SANDWICH

An American classic, the club sandwich traditionally includes bacon and chicken, and is made with toasted bread. This unconventional vegetarian version is packed full of ingredients with wonderful flavours, such as pesto, goat's cheese, roasted peppers, and balsamic vinegar. It proves that tradition need not always be respected when you have imagination.

INGREDIENTS

12 slices quality crusty white bread
2 red peppers, roasted, peeled, deseeded (see page 39), and cut in strips
4 hard-boiled eggs, peeled and sliced
handful watercress or rocket leaves
2 plum tomatoes, sliced
¼ cucumber, thinly sliced
1 small red onion, thinly sliced
4 tbsp balsamic vinegar
salt and freshly ground pepper

FOR THE GOAT'S CHEESE PESTO

1 garlic clove, crushed
handful fresh basil leaves
1 tbsp pine kernels
100ml (3½fl oz) olive oil
1 tbsp freshly grated Parmesan
40g (1½oz) soft mild goat's cheese

1 For the pesto, blend the garlic, basil, and pine kernels to a purée in a blender or food processor, gradually adding the oil as you blend. Add the cheeses, blend, and season.

2 Spread 8 slices of bread thickly with pesto on one side. Lay 4 slices of bread on a work surface, pesto-side up. Scatter the peppers over them, followed by the egg and watercress. Top each sandwich with another slice of bread, pesto-side up.

3 Arrange a layer of tomatoes, cucumber, and red onion on top. Season, then sprinkle with the vinegar. Top each sandwich with a plain slice of bread. Serve cut into triangles.

Preparation time
50 minutes

Serves 4

Nutritional notes
kcalories 637; protein 21g; carbohydrate 54g; total fat 39g, of which saturated fat 8g; fibre 4g; sodium 780mg

PAN BAGNAT

Pan Bagnat, which means "bathed bread" in French, is a healthy, filling Provençal sandwich, made with bread moistened with olive oil. Based on the recipe for a Niçoise salad, it is filled with wonderfully colourful ingredients and makes ideal picnic fare. Be sure to use good-quality olive oil for this recipe.

INGREDIENTS

4 ciabatta rolls or large baps
4 garlic cloves, halved
8 tbsp olive oil
200g (7oz) French beans, blanched
4 small tomatoes, quartered
2 small red onions, chopped
16 pitted black olives
8 quail's eggs, hard-boiled, peeled, and halved
4 small red peppers, roasted, peeled, deseeded (see page 39), and cut in strips
salt and freshly ground pepper

FOR THE DRESSING

125ml (4fl oz) olive oil
4 tbsp balsamic vinegar
1 tbsp chopped fresh basil

1 Cut the ciabatta rolls or baps in half, then rub the insides of the rolls with the cut faces of the garlic and brush with oil.

2 Cut the French beans into 2cm (¾ inch) lengths. Place the tomatoes, onions, beans, olives, quail's eggs, and peppers in a bowl. Blend together the oil, vinegar, and basil and drizzle this dressing over the ingredients in the bowl. Toss well and season to taste.

3 Divide the salad ingredients equally between the four ciabatta halves. Top with the remaining ciabatta halves and press down firmly. Serve immediately.

Preparation time
50 minutes

Serves 4

Nutritional notes
kcalories 743; protein 11g; carbohydrate 42g; total fat 60g, of which saturated fat 9g; fibre 7g; sodium 1183mg

MENU PLANNER

WHEN PLANNING A MEAL, YOU SHOULD
CONSIDER SEVERAL ELEMENTS: THE
NUMBER OF GUESTS, THEIR INDIVIDUAL
TASTES, THE AVAILABILITY OF
INGREDIENTS AND, MOST IMPORTANTLY,
WHAT YOU ARE HAPPY COOKING.
HERE ARE A FEW SUGGESTIONS TO HELP
MAKE ANY OCCASION — FROM A GARDEN
PARTY TO A FAMILY GET-TOGETHER —
A VERY SUCCESSFUL ONE.

FAMILY-STYLE SUPPER

These are wholesome dishes that everyone can
enjoy, followed by an indulgent pudding
that will keep any family happy. Children love
the cheesy crust of the vegetable pie.

CHICKPEA & CHARD MINESTRONE
page 60

ROOT VEGETABLE PIE WITH
POLENTA CRUST
page 88

HAZELNUT TORTE
WITH KIRSCH & BLUEBERRIES
page 126

ABOVE *Root Vegetable Pie with Polenta Crust*
LEFT *Hazelnut Torte with Kirsch & Blueberries*

ONE-POT MEALS

This is an almost effortless way to entertain your guests. Choose one of these one-pot meals and serve it with bread and perhaps a salad for a satisfying lunch or supper.

MARDI GRAS JAMBALAYA
page 98

CAULIFLOWER & LENTIL PALAK
page 91

VEGETARIAN PAELLA
page 102

RIGHT *Mardi Gras Jambalaya*

WARMING, COMFORTING SUPPER

Comfort foods should contain the familiar flavours of childhood. Cold winter nights were made for these robust, old-fashioned dishes, full of soothing carbohydrates.

PARSNIP & WILD RICE
MULLIGATAWNY
page 61

HUNGARIAN STEW
WITH CARAWAY DUMPLINGS
page 96

OATMEAL TREACLE TART
page 133

LEFT *Hungarian Stew with Caraway Dumplings*

GARDEN PARTY

Hot summer days demand vibrant flavours
and light dishes that can be prepared in advance.
This menu is perfect for days that are too
hot to spend slaving over the oven.

GREQUE OF VEGETABLES
WITH HERB CHEESE
page 53

LAZY CARIBBEAN SOUP
page 58

VEGETABLE SHASHLIKS ON TABBOULEH
page 149

CHOCOLATE & CHILLI OIL TART
page 130

LEFT *Lazy Caribbean Soup*

LIGHT & HEALTHY

If you are looking for a light meal, but still
want to spoil your guests, try this sophisticated
menu that is low in calories but packed
with extravagant flavours.

HOT & SOUR VEGETABLE SOUP
page 67

POLENTA VERDE WITH
WILD MUSHROOMS
page 105

SAFFRON PEACHES WITH
SUMMER BERRIES
page 124

RIGHT *Saffron Peaches with Summer Berries*

ROMANTIC DINNER

The starter and dessert can be prepared in advance, so you can relax and enjoy them with your loved one. The risotto is the only thing that needs last-minute attention.

LAYERED MEDITERRANEAN
GATEAU WITH LABNA
page 48

THAI-INSPIRED RISOTTO
WITH PUMPKIN
page 101

ITALIAN CREME CARAMEL
page 135

LEFT *Layered Mediterranean Gâteau with Labna*

DINNER PARTY

Dinner with friends should be an informal occasion, when you do not need to stand on ceremony and can indulge people's tastes, or try out unusual recipes.

GOAT'S CHEESE LATKES WITH
BEETROOT SALSA
page 50

CEP, WALNUT & JERUSALEM
ARTICHOKE PARCELS
page 73

BUTTERNUT SOUFFLE
WITH BLACKBERRIES
page 131

RIGHT *Cep, Walnut & Jerusalem Artichoke Parcels*

BUFFET SUPPER

A buffet table should be generously laden
with food, attractively presented, and easy to serve.

CHILLI-MARINATED OLIVES, GUACAMOLE
& CHEESE CHALUPAS *pages 56 & 57*

GRILLED VEGETABLE GAZPACHO *page 63*

HIGH-RISE PASTA PIE *page 71*

PURPLE POTATO, ARTICHOKE
& MILLET SALAD *page 122*

SINGAPORE NOODLE SALAD *page 120*

GREEN LEAF SALAD
WITH GARDEN HERBS *page 123*

PROSECCO-MASCARPONE &
RASPBERRY SYLLABUB *page 127*

LEFT *Grilled Vegetable Gazpacho*

NEW MED MAGIC

Inspired by the sun-drenched flavours of the Eastern
Mediterranean, this spread makes a dazzling
summer dinner that tastes best if eaten outdoors.

MIDDLE EASTERN
FLATBREAD & SUMAK SALAD
page 121

GREEK BABY VEGETABLES
WITH ORZO
page 106

CANDIED AUBERGINE
& CARDAMOM ICE-CREAM
page 135

RIGHT *Greek Baby Vegetables with Orzo*

SPRING IS IN THE AIR

Spring is a time to serve light dishes using tender young produce such as asparagus, broad beans, and rhubarb. Use simple cooking methods to maximize their fresh flavours.

GRILLED ASPARAGUS WITH GREMOLATA
page 51

PENNE WITH BROCCOLI & BROAD BEAN PESTO
page 82

APPLE & RHUBARB PIZZA WITH RHUBARB SORBET
page 128

LEFT *Apple & Rhubarb Pizza with Rhubarb Sorbet*

LAZY SUNDAY

Brunch is a relaxed occasion, easy on both the cook and the guests. Serve plenty of Buck's Fizz and provide the Sunday papers for those who do not like conversation in the morning.

MY FAVOURITE MUESLI
page 141

SIMPLE HUEVOS RANCHEROS
page 136

BLUEBERRY PANCAKES WITH MAPLE SYRUP
page 139

RIGHT *Simple Huevos Rancheros*

INDEX

ACKNOWLEDGMENTS

AUTHOR'S ACKNOWLEDGMENTS
The author would like to thank:
my family, for their support and
understanding that a chef's life can
be demanding, hectic, and somewhat
unsociable. Philip Lamb, one of my
Chefs de Partie at the Lanesborough,
who has been instrumental in
helping me test and taste the recipes.
I thank him for his help, support,
and most importantly, his patience.
Jane Suthering, food stylist, friend
and respected professional, and

Philip Wilkins, photographer:
this is our second book together and
hopefully not our last. Between them
their expertise never fails to amaze
me. I thank them for bringing the
food to life in their own inimitable
way. Jo Younger, Project Editor, for
her superb editing of my recipes. Her
warmth and good nature, friendship
and patience have been greatly
appreciated. I cannot thank her
enough, and I hope I wasn't too
much trouble. Nicky Vimpany, for

her help also with the editing.
Julia Worth, for her wonderful
design concept for this book, which
I believe brings the whole thing
together in harmony. Danny Murphy
of Chef's Connection, for giving me
such lovely produce to work with on
a daily basis. Jane Middleton, for all
her help. Fiona Lyndsey and Linda
Shanks, my agents, who still manage
to find enough work to fill my spare
time so that I don't get too bored.
Daphne Razazan, Editorial Director

at DK, for giving me the opportunity
to express how interesting and
innovative vegetarian cooking can be.

PUBLISHER'S ACKNOWLEDGMENTS
Dorling Kindersley would like
to thank: Mary Ling, for initial
editorial planning; Lorraine Turner,
for editorial assistance; Pat Bacon,
for nutritional information; Brigid
Land, for photographic assistance;
Emma Patmore, for additional
home economy.